ChatGPT Essentials for Beginners (2024)

Revolutionize your everyday life and the life of your small business with ChatGPT!

James Gilbert

Simera Publishing

Book Cover by Milan Krstevski

Contents

Dedication

"To service, providence and freedom"

Introduction

Have you ever found yourself stuck on a seemingly unsolvable problem, wishing for a genie to offer an instant solution? Well, that genie exists and is more accessible than you think. Imagine harnessing a tool that revolutionizes the way you tackle daily personal challenges, streamlines your business operations, and offers a competitive edge in a world driven by innovation. That tool is ChatGPT! ChatGPT is an artificial intelligence (AI) program, a chatbot, that generates dialogue. It was developed by AI research company OpenAI in 2015. AI is a technology that uses natural language processing (NLP) to enable computers and machines to conduct human-like conversations and simulate human intelligence and problem-solving capabilities. ChatGPT is not another tech buzzword; it is a transformative ally for individuals and small businesses, poised to redefine productivity and creativity.

This book will introduce you to cutting-edge technology and guide you in transforming your daily tasks and business processes with unparalleled ease and efficiency. By embracing ChatGPT, you will keep abreast with technology by propelling yourself and your business into a future where challenges are met with smart, efficient, tailored solutions.

ChatGPT's uniqueness lies in its versatility, accessibility, and ability to be customized to meet your needs. This book will demonstrate how ChatGPT can be your partner in navigating the complexities of modern life and business through effective, innovative, time-saving solutions.

The ChatGPT journey begins in Chapter 1 with the foundational knowledge necessary to understand ChatGPT's capabilities and its potential impact on your life and work. Then, in Chapter 2, we will explore how to customize the ChatGPT NLP model to suit your personal or business needs.

In Chapter 3, we will look into how ChatGPT can boost personal efficiency. This chapter offers practical advice and step-by-step guidelines for harnessing ChatGPT for personal growth.

Next, we will learn in Chapter 4 how to leverage ChatGPT for small businesses. This discussion focuses on the transformational potential of ChatGPT in the small business realm. It covers everything from customer service automation and content creation to data analysis and decision-making support, and it provides actionable strategies for businesses seeking to innovate and thrive.

We will then move on to the advanced capabilities of ChatGPT. Chapter 6 addresses custom models and integration with other software and explores cutting-edge uses of ChatGPT in various industries.

The ethical considerations and future outlooks of ChatGPT are addressed in Chapter 6, where we will demonstrate the potential boundaries and limits of ChatGPT and the importance of maintaining realistic expectations about its capabilities. It also addresses the unethical use of AI and describes the anticipated future of such technology. This chapter reflects on privacy concerns and the dangers of ChatGPT, and it offers insights into the evolving landscape of AI to prepare you for what's ahead.

Finally, in Chapter 8, we provide examples of practical, useful ChatGPT prompts for both personal use and use by small businesses. ChatGPT prompts are the specific instructions or queries given to ChatGPT to generate the users' desired response.

As you read this book, engage with ChatGPT, experiment with it, and apply what you learn to your personal and business activities. Let each chapter inspire you to investigate new ways of leveraging ChatGPT and push the boundaries of what you thought possible. Whether you seek to streamline your workflow, amplify your business operations, or satisfy your curiosity about the potential of AI, now is the time to act. Join us on this journey of discovery and empowerment. The future is here, waiting for you to seize it.

Chapter One

Foundations of ChatGPT

In a bustling small town, Sarah runs her dream business: a coffee shop. Amidst the aroma of freshly brewed coffee, she juggles everything from serving customers to managing supplies. But as her business grows, so do her challenges. She often finds herself swamped, wishing for a way to manage her expanding workload without hiring more staff—a costly solution she wants to delay.

As an alternative, Sarah integrates artificial intelligence (AI) into her business. AI is a technology that uses natural language processing (NLP) to enable computers and machines to conduct human-like conversations and simulate human intelligence and problem-solving capabilities. Sarah uses AI by delegating to ChatGPT such tasks as answering customer queries and planning her supply orders. The difference it makes is not just visible; it's transformative. Sarah's coffee shop runs smoother, her customers are happier, and she even finds time to experiment with new coffee blends, something she's always wanted to do.

This story isn't unique to Sarah or her coffee shop. Across the globe, individuals and business owners face similar hurdles every day. The introduction of ChatGPT into their operations opens a new world of possibilities for growth and success. The impact of integrating ChatGPT into everyday life and business is profound. For Sarah, it isn't just about answering customer queries or managing orders; it's about unlocking potential she didn't know her business had. ChatGPT allows Sarah to focus on what she loves most about her coffee shop: creating new blends and engaging with her community.

What makes ChatGPT particularly exciting is its adaptability. If you're looking to enhance productivity, boost creativity, or improve customer engagement, ChatGPT can be tailored to meet all of these needs. Its foundation in NLP means it can understand nuances and context, providing responses and solutions that are both relevant and personalized.

Understanding ChatGPT's Role in NLP

ChatGPT exemplifies the pinnacle of what NLP can achieve: transforming our interactions with technology by understanding and generating human-like text. But how is this bridge between the complex world of NLP and our everyday digital conversations built? Let's break it down into simple terms.

ChatGPT, at its core, is like a master linguist, fluent in the language of humans and computers alike. This fluency is about recognizing words and understanding intentions, emotions, and nuances behind what we say or type. Imagine telling a friend a joke and the friend laughing in response. You and the friend don't just share words; you share understanding and connection. ChatGPT aims to digitally replicate this level of comprehension and make our interactions with machines feel more natural and human.

Now, you may wonder: How does ChatGPT manage this feat? The secret comes from its training. ChatGPT reads millions of books, conversations, and articles. From this vast ocean of text, it learns how language works, not just grammar and vocabulary but the subtler aspects, such as how to tell a story, answer a question, or offer advice. When you ask ChatGPT a question, it doesn't just search for a pre-written answer. Instead, it draws on everything it has read and learned to craft a response just for you, composing a short text on the spot.

This capability makes ChatGPT incredibly versatile. Need a quick summary of a complex topic? ChatGPT can help. Looking for creative ideas for a story or project? ChatGPT's got your back. Struggling with a math problem? Yes, ChatGPT can assist there too.

But let's not stop at *what* ChatGPT can do. Let's also consider *how* it does these things. When ChatGPT processes your input, it scans an expansive collection of data for keywords or phrases and interprets your intent. This process involves a sophisticated dance of algorithms and models, all working to understand the context and meaning behind your words. It's akin to piecing together a puzzle, whereby each word or phrase is a puzzle piece, and the picture formed by the completed puzzle is your intent. ChatGPT uses its understanding of language to assemble pieces of information into a coherent, appropriate response.

To understand the ChatGPT process, visualize a chef creating a dish from a recipe. Just as the chef uses knowledge of flavors and cooking techniques to bring a recipe to life, ChatGPT uses its knowledge of language to turn your input into meaningful output. And just as a skilled chef can modify a dish to suit your taste, ChatGPT can tailor its responses to fit your needs and preferences.

One may ask: Why is all this important? The answer is the potential that ChatGPT unlocks. With ChatGPT, technology becomes more accessible, intuitive, and helpful. ChatGPT is about making machines smarter and enhancing our ability to communicate, learn, and create. In a world in which technology is increasingly intertwined with every aspect of our lives, tools like ChatGPT help bridge the gap between human creativity and computational power, making the digital world a natural extension of our human experience.

ChatGPT's relevance extends beyond individual tasks. It's also shaping the future of education, work, and creativity. Educators use it to inspire students and personalize learning. Businesses employ it to improve customer service and streamline operations. Creatives leverage it to look into new ideas and express themselves in novel ways. In each of these cases, ChatGPT acts as a catalyst, enhancing human efforts with machine intelligence.

The Transformative Impact of NLP for the Road Ahead

NLP stands as a beacon of accessibility and innovation. NLP-powered tools are tearing down the barriers that once made technology seem distant and complex. Today, anyone can converse with digital devices and services in their natural language and make technology a more integrated part of our everyday lives. This leap in accessibility means that more people than ever can leverage technology to learn, create, and communicate. The essence of this revolution comes from making our interactions with technology as natural and effortless as speaking to a friend.

As we look to the future, the potential advancements in NLP hold promise for an even more seamless integration of technology into our lives. Through the continuous improvement of algorithms and models, NLP is set to offer a deeper understanding of human language's subtleties. Future iterations likely will grasp not solely the words we use but the emotions, intentions, and nuances behind them. This evolution will enable technology to provide more personalized, context-aware responses, making interactions with digital assistants and services seem even more like interactions with human beings.

In the future, we could see iterations of NLP bridge every linguistic and cultural gap, enabling effortless communication across the globe. Innovations could include real-time translation services that allow people to converse without language barriers, educational tools that adapt to each student's unique learning style, and customer service bots that understand and address the emotional context of inquiries. These advancements will make technology an even more empowering and unifying force in our society.

Furthermore, as NLP becomes more sophisticated, we can anticipate its integration into a broader range of applications. These range from healthcare, for which NLP could interpret patient data to offer personalized care recommendations, to the creative industries, wherein NLP could inspire artists and writers with suggestions and insights drawn from vast datasets. The possibilities are as limitless as our imagination, pointing toward a future in which technology understands us deeply and contributes to our lives in ever more meaningful ways.

NLP is at the forefront of a paradigm shift in our relationship with technology. By making digital interactions more natural, intuitive, and human-like, NLP is enhancing our present by paving the way for a future in which technology's potential will be fully aligned with the richness of human communication. As we look forward, the evolution of NLP promises to take us to a world where technology speaks our language, understands our needs, and enriches our lives in unprecedented ways. The exploration of NLP is far from over, and its future shines bright with the promise of bringing us closer to an environment in which technology truly understands and serves humanity.

Introduction to ChatGPT Models

The process toward the creation of ChatGPT 3.5 encompassed several earlier versions, with each iteration having moved us closer to enabling machines to comprehend and respond to human queries with unprecedented accuracy and nuance. Each step forward in ChatGPT's evolution brought sharper understanding, more coherent responses, and a broader knowledge base, laying the groundwork for the more advanced capabilities of ChatGPT 3.5.

Why focus on ChatGPT 3.5? you may wonder. The choice of ChatGPT 3.5 is both deliberate and significant. This ChatGPT version stands out due to its wide availability at no cost, making it the most accessible version for individuals and small business owners. Its widespread use is a testament to not only its affordability but also its versatility and effectiveness across various applications.

ChatGPT 3.5 represents a significant leap forward in NLP technology. This version is not merely about a machine understanding human words and sentences; it's about grasping context, interpreting nuances, and generating responses that seem intuitively human. This version has refined its predecessors' capabilities, offering an enhanced understanding of context, improved accuracy, and a comprehensive knowledge base that spans a vast array of topics and subjects.

The implications of this refinement are profound. With ChatGPT 3.5, the barrier between human and machine communication is more blurred than ever before. Drafting an email, composing a poem, solving a complex math problem, or providing customer service can be handled by ChatGPT 3.5 with a finesse that rivals human capability. This model has democratized access to advanced AI, enabling users from diverse backgrounds to leverage cutting-edge technology in their daily lives and work.

This democratization extends to the small business owner who uses ChatGPT 3.5 to automate customer inquiries, freeing up valuable time to focus on other aspects of their business, as well as to students who rely on it to break down complex scientific concepts into digestible explanations. The applications are as varied as the users, showcasing the model's adaptability and broad utility.

The benefits of ChatGPT 3.5 extend beyond its functionality. Making such powerful technology freely available opens new avenues for innovation and creativity. Individuals and businesses can experiment with AI and integrate it into their operations without substantial investment in technology or expertise. This accessibility is a game changer, leveling the playing field and fostering a culture of innovation and exploration.

As we look ahead, the future of ChatGPT models is bright with potential. As NLP technology evolves, we can anticipate models that offer an even greater understanding of human language, more personalized interactions, and applications that stretch the boundaries of today's imagination. The ongoing development promises to improve our relationship with technology, making our interactions more natural, intuitive, and, ultimately, more human.

Addressing Accessibility with ChatGPT 3.5

The world of advanced technology, particularly in the realm of NLP, has often been perceived as a field accessible only to those with deep pockets or specialized knowledge. However, ChatGPT 3.5 shatters this notion by bringing this sophisticated technology to everyone, free of charge. Its role in democratizing access to cutting-edge AI cannot be overstated.

Consider the implications of this accessibility. Small businesses, for example, can now harness the power of advanced AI without significant investment. This levels the playing field, allowing them to compete with larger entities that traditionally have had more resources to invest in technology. Similarly, educators, students, and independent creators can integrate AI into their work, fostering innovation and creativity.

The free availability of ChatGPT 3.5 means that anyone with an internet connection and a device can start experimenting with this technology. It's just like giving a powerful digital tool to a wide array of artisans, each of whom will use it in unique and creative ways, pushing the boundaries of what's possible in their respective fields.

Future Directions

The current capabilities of ChatGPT 3.5 are just the tip of the iceberg. Future enhancements could include a more nuanced understanding of language, greater contextual awareness, and the ability to seamlessly integrate with a wide array of applications.

Users and enthusiasts must stay informed about these advancements. As the technology evolves, so too will the opportunities for applying it. Ongoing innovation in NLP and AI promises to continually expand the horizons of what we can achieve with tools like ChatGPT, opening doors to new possibilities in every field, from education to business to art and beyond.

ChatGPT 3.5, with its wide accessibility and advanced capabilities, is an ever-evolving tool creating a stepping stone to a future where AI and human creativity come together in synergy. This technology is not an endpoint but a path forward, leading us to a world where the language of machines and humans intertwine in a dance of progress and possibility.

Now that we have laid a solid foundation for understanding ChatGPT and its incredible capabilities we will shift our focus from the what to the how in Chapter 2, which will guide you through setting up and integrating ChatGPT into your daily routines and business operations. Get ready to transform your understanding into action and unlock the full potential of this revolutionary tool in your everyday life and business ventures!

Chapter Two

ChatGPT Setup for Individuals and Small Businesses

In this chapter, we dive into how you can set up and adjust ChatGPT 3.5 to fit into your day-to-day life or small business. Are you seeking to enhance personal productivity? Streamline business processes? Explore the innovative world of AI? This chapter will provide step-by-step instructions, practical tips, and insightful strategies to effectively harness the power of ChatGPT for these purposes and more.

Most users of ChatGPT are not looking for a generic setup; they want a setup tailor-made to their needs and wants. This chapter is your guide to making ChatGPT 3.5 an indispensable part of your routine, helping you tackle time-consuming and challenging tasks more efficiently and effectively.

Now let's talk about personalizing ChatGPT for your daily use. We all have unique preferences for the ways in which we like to receive our information. Some of us prefer quick, straight-to-the-point answers, while others favor more detailed explanations. ChatGPT 3.5 is a tool that understands the nuances of your business or your personal life, and lets you incorporate your preferences into the program.

In personal use, this level of customization means ChatGPT can assist you with everything from planning your day to helping you learn a new skill. The functions of ChatGPT mimic having a personal assistant who knows exactly what you need, such as reminders to conduct important tasks or help with researching a topic you're curious about. For instance, if you love cooking, you can tailor ChatGPT to give you recipe ideas and cooking tips or even create a weekly meal plan. If you're into fitness, ChatGPT can be your go-to for workout routines or tracking progress.

For small businesses, ChatGPT approaches customization from a different angle by aligning with your business' voice and needs. If you run a boutique, ChatGPT can handle customer queries on sizes, colors, and stock availability in a tone that matches your brand's style. Or if you're in a tech-related field, it can assist with technical support queries by using the language specific to your industry. For some businesses, alignment may mean training ChatGPT to recognize and respond to customers' common questions.

And here's the best part: experimenting with different settings in ChatGPT 3.5 is easy and risk-free. You can try different configurations until you find the setup that suits you best. Think of it as tuning an instrument until it plays the perfect melody for your needs.

Remember that the power of ChatGPT 3.5 is grounded in its flexibility and adaptability. It's a tool that can grow and change with you; for personal tasks or as a part of your business operations. The goal is to make your life easier and more efficient, and with the right setup, ChatGPT 3.5 is more than up to the task.

So, take the knowledge from this chapter and start exploring. Set up ChatGPT 3.5 to work for you and see the difference it makes in your day-to-day life or business. The possibilities are endless, but they all start with the same first step: customization.

ChatGPT 3.5 Customization Basics

To reiterate, the power of ChatGPT 3.5 lies in its ability to be customized. Customization transforms ChatGPT 3.5 from a general AI tool into a personalized assistant or a tailored business solution. Customization allows users to shape AI's responses and functionalities to fit their specific needs, making it a versatile tool for anyone.

The path to unlock ChatGPT 3.5's full potential begins with accessing its customization features. To get started, log into your ChatGPT account. This is a straightforward process, much like logging on into any other online service. Once you are logged in, the path to customization is accessed by navigating to the right spot in ChatGPT. Your account name will be visible on the platform. Click on your account name to reveal the option labeled "Custom Instructions," which will open a customization menu. This menu is the gateway to a world of possibilities for tailoring ChatGPT to individual preferences.

Upon entering the customization menu, you will be greeted by an array of options. Here, you can set preferences for language style, tone, and specific areas of knowledge or expertise. For instance, you may prefer responses in a formal tone, or perhaps you need for ChatGPT to have a grasp of medical terminology for professional purposes. These settings are not entirely cosmetic; they fundamentally alter how ChatGPT interacts with you as the user, aligning with your specific needs and the context you prefer.

Consider a scenario: a teacher is looking to use ChatGPT as a tool for creating educational content. By setting preferences for ChatGPT to understand educational jargon and communicate in a friendly tone, it becomes an invaluable assistant in crafting lesson plans or explaining complex concepts in a student-friendly manner.

Customizing ChatGPT 3.5 is not about just ticking boxes or selecting options. It molds the AI to fit the unique contours of the user's requirements. For anyone from a business owner who wants to automate customer interactions, to a student seeking help with academic research, the ability to customize ChatGPT ensures that it can effectively serve a wide range of purposes specific to the user. As a user navigates the customization settings, it's crucial to experiment and find the right combination that suits that user's needs. The platform is designed to be user-friendly, allowing even those who are not tech-savvy to make adjustments with ease.

In essence, the customization of ChatGPT 3.5 is about creating a tool that understands what the user wants and responds in the most beneficial way to that user. From refining the AI to provide quick, concise answers for a busy professional to setting it up to offer detailed, in-depth responses for a curious learner, the flexibility of ChatGPT 3.5 makes it a valuable asset in a variety of scenarios.

Customization for Personal Use

Let's dive into the types of customizations that can make a real difference to the user, like tone customizations. ChatGPT's tone can be friendly, professional, humorous, or straightforward; it's all about what suits your style. For instance, if you're asking ChatGPT to brainstorm ideas for your next novel, a friendly, creative tone will be ideal. Or if you need help with professional emails, a formal tone will work best.

Next up, after setting the tone, is aligning ChatGPT with your interests. If you're a tech enthusiast, a literature lover, or a fitness fanatic, ChatGPT can be tailored to talk about these topics with depth and understanding. For tech enthusiasts, it can stay updated on the latest gadgets and tech news, while for literature lovers, it can discuss classic novels or even suggest new reads.

Another vital customization is the response style. Some users prefer quick, concise answers, while others enjoy detailed explanations. For someone who's always on the go, brief responses to queries on weather updates or news summaries can be incredibly handy. Conversely, if you're planning a detailed project such as a home renovation, more elaborate responses with step-by-step guidance can be useful.

But how do you make these customizations? It's simple. Within the ChatGPT interface, you'll find options to set your preferences. With a few clicks, you can change how ChatGPT talks to you, what it talks about, and the depth of information it provides.

Consider a few scenarios in which customizations would come into play. If you're learning a new language, ChatGPT can become your practice partner, conversing with you in the language you're learning and providing corrections and suggestions. For those interested in staying fit, it can suggest daily workout routines and healthy recipes and provide motivation.

The benefits of these customizations are immense. They save time by providing information that's directly relevant to you, make daily tasks easier, and help you learn new skills. By tailoring ChatGPT to your personal needs, you get a tool that understands and assists you in your everyday life.

These personal touches make ChatGPT not just a tool, but a companion that understands your needs and preferences. From helping with your hobbies, to managing your daily tasks, ChatGPT is there to make every day a little easier, more organized, and a lot more enjoyable.

So, take the time to familiarize yourself with these customization options. Play around with the settings, try different combinations, and see how ChatGPT can fit into various aspects of your life. With a bit of modification, ChatGPT can become an integral part of your daily routine, making your day-to-day tasks smoother and your projects more fulfilling.

Customization for Small Businesses

In today's fast-paced business world, small businesses need every advantage they can get, and ChatGPT offers just that. Customization of ChatGPT for small businesses is not just a luxury; it's a necessity for staying competitive and relevant. Tailored settings in ChatGPT can meet specific business needs, streamline operations, and siqnificantly amplify customer interactions.

For small businesses, customization options in ChatGPT can be a game-changer. The first step is to align the AI's tone with the business' brand voice. Whether your brand is professional, casual, or somewhere in between, ChatGPT can mirror this tone, ensuring consistency in customer interactions. For instance, a boutique with a friendly, conversational style can set ChatGPT to interact with customers in a similar manner, making the shopping experience more personal and engaging.

Another critical aspect of customization for a small business is to set up industry specific knowledge. Every industry has its jargon and nuances, and ChatGPT can be customized to understand this language and use it effectively. This customization makes ChatGPT your trusted ally, especially in providing accurate and relevant responses to customer inquiries.

Tailoring ChatGPT for customer service tasks is another area where small businesses can reap significant benefits. From handling frequently asked questions (FAQs) to providing detailed product information, ChatGPT can manage various customer service tasks, freeing up valuable time for the business owner and employees.

Implementing these customizations is a straightforward task. Within the ChatGPT platform, business owners can access settings to adjust the tone, add industry-specific terms, and set up automated responses for common customer inquiries. These adjustments are not about altering a few settings; they're about transforming ChatGPT into an integral part of the business' customer service team.

Let's look at some real-life examples:

- A small retail store specializing in handmade goods used ChatGPT to answer common customer queries about product materials and care instructions. By customizing the AI to understand and use specific terms related to their products, the store became equipped to provide accurate information, which improved customer satisfaction and trust.

- A marketing agency leveraged ChatGPT for content creation. By customizing the AI to understand their brand voice and industry jargon, the agency generated consistent, high-quality content and significantly reduced the time and effort involved in content creation.

- A tech start-up used ChatGPT for technical support. By feeding the AI with industry-specific knowledge and terms, the start-up provided efficient, accurate technical assistance to their customers, enhancing their reputation for superior customer service.

The benefits of these customizations are self-evident. For the retail store, there was a noticeable increase in customer satisfaction and a reduction in the time staff spent answering routine questions. The marketing agency saw a boost in content production efficiency, allowing them to focus on more creative aspects of their business. And the tech startup improved its customer service quality, which increased customer loyalty and generated positive reviews.

For small businesses, customizing ChatGPT means more than just adjusting a digital tool; it's about creating a unique solution that caters to their specific business needs. ChatGPT's customization options open a world of possibilities, from enhancing customer service, streamlining content creation, or providing accurate industry-specific information.

Owners of small businesses are encouraged to experiment with ChatGPT's customization features, with the goal of finding the perfect balance that fits their business model and enhances their operations. With ChatGPT, small businesses can innovate, improve efficiency, and offer a level of customer service that sets them apart from the competition.

ChatGPT 3.5 is a tool for today and an investment in your future. It's a versatile solution that can significantly change your day-to-day life and business operations. As you move forward in this rapidly evolving digital landscape, continuous exploration and adaptation of AI tools like ChatGPT 3.5 are essential. These tools will keep you ahead of your competitors, ensuring that you remain efficient, effective and competitive in your industry.

Your exploration into ChatGPT 3.5 is just beginning. With each customization and every use, you will discover more about its capabilities and, in turn, your potential to innovate and improve. So, take what you've learned in this chapter and start exploring. Shape ChatGPT 3.5 to your world, and watch as it transforms how you work, learn, and play.

Chapter Three

Leveraging ChatGPT for Personal Use

In a world where time is as precious as gold, finding ways to get more tasks done is extremely important. In this chapter, we will unlock the secrets of using ChatGPT to supercharge your personal productivity.

If you're struggling to keep up with your daily tasks, looking for ways to boost your learning, or curious about how AI can fit into your personal life, this chapter has you covered. We'll dive into the practical applications of ChatGPT, showing you how it can be your personal assistant, tutor, creative partner, and so much more.

From automating routine tasks to generating new ideas for your hobbies, from planning your meals to solving unexpected problems, ChatGPT is the Swiss Army knife in your digital toolbox. And the best part? You don't need to be a tech wizard to use it. With straightforward commands and a bit of creativity, you'll see how ChatGPT can make your life more efficient and enjoyable.

So, let's get started. By the end of this chapter, you'll see how integrating ChatGPT into your daily routine can save you time, reduce stress, and spark a bit of joy in the otherwise mundane.

Applications of ChatGPT in Personal Settings: Learning and Research

In the quest for knowledge, everyone seeks a reliable, always-available source of information. ChatGPT steps into this role perfectly by acting as an infinite library at your fingertips. However, ChatGPT doesn't just give you quick answers, it transforms how you learn and conduct research, making the quest for knowledge easier and more engaging.

With ChatGPT, the barriers to learning new topics and diving deep into research become dramatically lower. No matter your question, ChatGPT is there to provide explanations, offer resources, or even guide you through complex concepts, step by step. This is not about replacing traditional learning methods; it's about enhancing them. ChatGPT can complement your studies by offering tailored explanations or suggesting new areas to explore, making learning a dynamic and interactive experience.

For students, professionals, and the curious, using ChatGPT is like having a tutor available around the clock, ready to answer your questions, help with homework, and provide insights on virtually any topic. It's incredibly valuable for those moments when you're stuck on a problem and need a new perspective. Just type in your question or query as a prompt at the bottom of your interface, and ChatGPT will offer a variety of approaches or solutions to help you break through those frustrating barriers to understanding.

Beyond academic learning, ChatGPT is a powerful tool for personal research projects. ChatGPT can help you gather information, brainstorm ideas, and make informed decisions, whether you are planning a trip, exploring a new hobby, or starting a side business. Its ability to pull from a wide range of sources means you get a well-rounded view of any subject you're interested in.

ChatGPT encourages you to ask questions you may not think to ask. It's like talking with someone who knows a lot about everything. This back-and-forth interaction can lead you down fascinating paths of inquiry you may not have explored otherwise, enriching your understanding of the world.

ChatGPT is revolutionizing the way we approach learning and research. It makes the pursuit of knowledge more interactive, accessible, and fun. If you're seeking to understand complex scientific theories, learn a new language, or discover more about your favorite historical period, ChatGPT stands ready to assist. It opens a world of knowledge with just a few keystrokes.

Task Automation with ChatGPT

The magic of ChatGPT extends into the realm of task automation, transforming the repetitive and mundane into the streamlined and simple. With its advanced capabilities, ChatGPT empowers users to automate a variety of tasks, from scheduling and reminders to data analysis and beyond, all with straightforward commands or scripts. This saves valuable time and increases efficiency, allowing more room for creativity and important tasks.

Scheduling and calendar management. Keeping track of appointments and meetings can be a breeze. By integrating ChatGPT with your calendar, you can set up reminders, add new events, or even reschedule appointments with text commands.

Social media management. For those who need to maintain a presence on social media, ChatGPT can automate posting schedules, generate content ideas, and even reply to frequently occurring comments, ensuring your profiles stay active and engaging without constant attention.

Shopping and to-do lists. With ChatGPT 3.5, you will never again forget to purchase a needed item. ChatGPT can help manage your shopping lists, suggest items based on past purchases, and track tasks, ensuring you stay organized and efficient.

Learning new skills. Yes, automation can extend to your personal growth. ChatGPT can curate learning resources, track your progress in acquiring new skills, or quiz you on learned material, making your journey to mastery more structured and less overwhelming.

Customized reminders. From watering plants to taking breaks, ChatGPT can remind you of small but important tasks throughout the day, ensuring nothing gets overlooked.

Personal finance management. Managing finances becomes simpler with ChatGPT. It can track expenses, provide budget suggestions, and even remind you of upcoming bills, helping you stay on top of your financial health.

The beauty of ChatGPT task automation is the technologies' adaptability. ChatGPT is a flexible, powerful tool for transforming how you approach task management as a busy professional looking to optimize your workflow, a student aiming to manage your studies more effectively, or someone who wants to better organize their daily routine. With just a few easy commands or scripts, you can automate various tasks, freeing up time for what truly matters and enhancing your overall productivity and efficiency.

Personal Assistant through ChatGPT

Harnessing the power of ChatGPT for personal assistance ushers in a new era of time management and organization. This advanced tool acts like a personal administrative assistant, adept at handling tasks that streamline your day, making life manageable and organized.

ChatGPT can set up your daily agenda, remind you of upcoming appointments, and reschedule meetings based on your priorities and availability. But it doesn't stop at scheduling. ChatGPT takes on the role of a personal aide capable of managing your emails by filtering out spam and highlighting important messages. It can draft replies to routine emails, saving you significant effort. This allows you to focus on emails that require your personal touch, ensuring that your communications remain thoughtful and personal.

Your virtual assistant is also your personal notetaker. During meetings or brainstorming sessions, ChatGPT can help take down key points, organize them coherently, and provide summaries. This ensures that no critical information is lost and that you always have clear, actionable notes at your fingertips.

Planning travel can often be tedious, but with ChatGPT, it becomes a hassle-free experience. From researching destinations to booking flights and accommodations, ChatGPT can handle the preliminary legwork, presenting options that fit your preferences and budget. It can even suggest itineraries based on your interests, making travel planning an exciting adventure rather than a daunting task.

For those who juggle multiple projects or lead busy lifestyles, ChatGPT can track project milestones, set reminders for deadlines, and provide progress updates. This level of project management ensures that you're always on top of your work, helping you meet deadlines easily and efficiently.

Moreover, ChatGPT can serve as your personal coach, by offering motivation and tracking your habits to help you reach your personal and professional goals. ChatGPT can help with fitness habits, learning a new skill, or productivity, providing daily check-ins, encouragement, and resources to support your journey.

Cooking and Recipes with ChatGPT

Transforming the routine task of meal planning into an exciting culinary adventure is one of the delightful surprises ChatGPT brings into the kitchen. This innovative tool becomes your personal chef, offering inspiration, recipes, and cooking tips right at your fingertips. It's like unlocking a collection of culinary secrets that turn everyday cooking into a creative and enjoyable experience.

ChatGPT simplifies the process of deciding what to cook. Gone are the days of flipping through cookbooks or scrolling endlessly through online recipes. With a straightforward prompt, ChatGPT can suggest meals based on the ingredients in your pantry, ensuring you can whip up delicious dishes without last-minute grocery trips.

But the magic doesn't stop at meal suggestions. ChatGPT can also tailor recipes to suit dietary preferences and restrictions. Whether you need to cater to a gluten-free diet, vegetarian lifestyle, or any other specific nutritional requirement, ChatGPT can filter recipes to meet your needs, making it easier than ever to enjoy meals that are both delicious and suitable for everyone at the table.

For those who want to expand their culinary skills, ChatGPT, when provided the correct prompts, can serve as a cooking tutor. It can break down complex recipes into simple, easy-to-follow steps, demystifying the art of cooking. From kneading the perfect dough to mastering the art of the perfect sear, ChatGPT can provide step-by-step guidance, making it possible for even novice cooks to tackle ambitious dishes with confidence.

What's more, ChatGPT can inject fun into meal planning by suggesting themed dinner nights or culinary challenges. With ChatGPT, you can embark on a culinary tour of the world from your kitchen, with ChatGPT suggesting recipes from different countries, complete with cultural background and serving suggestions. It's an engaging way to learn about new cuisines and spice up daily meal prep.

And for those moments when you're in a rush, ChatGPT can come to the rescue with quick, easy recipes that can be prepared in minutes. These fast fixes ensure that a busy schedule doesn't mean compromising on a healthy and hearty meal. ChatGPT can even provide tips on meal prepping, helping you organize your food preparation for the week, saving time, and ensuring you always have something tasty and ready to eat.

In the world of cooking and recipes, ChatGPT can act as your culinary assistant, transforming meal preparation from a chore into a delightful exploration of flavors and dishes. It offers a blend of creativity, convenience, and learning, making every meal an opportunity to discover something new. If you're a seasoned chef or just beginning to cook, ChatGPT makes cooking an adventure worth savoring.

Idea Generation with ChatGPT

Unlocking the floodgates of creativity and innovation, ChatGPT stands out as a muse for those seeking fresh ideas for diverse projects.

In the realm of writing, ChatGPT can be transformed into a collaborative partner, offering plot twists for novelists, punchlines for scriptwriters, and compelling narratives for bloggers. With ChatGPT, writers break through the dreaded writer's block, discovering new directions and possibilities for their work.

For entrepreneurs and innovators, ChatGPT acts as a brainstorming ally. It helps in fleshing out business ideas, suggesting unique selling points, and identifying potential challenges and solutions. Startups can harness this tool to refine their business models, access untapped markets, or generate creative marketing strategies. ChatGPT's vast knowledge base and unbiased perspective serve as fertile ground for cultivating groundbreaking ideas that stand out in competitive landscapes.

Designers and artists, too, find a source of inspiration in ChatGPT. It can aid in conceptualizing art projects, suggesting design themes or offering historical context that enriches creative work.

Educators and students leverage ChatGPT for educational innovation, generating ideas for projects, lessons, and research topics. It becomes a tool for making learning more engaging, helping to design experiments, simulations, or interactive assignments that captivate and educate simultaneously.

Moreover, ChatGPT can be invaluable for problem-solving across various fields. It offers a multitude of perspectives on any challenge, encouraging out-of-the-box thinking that leads to novel solutions, unlocking effective and innovative answers to complex problems.

The beauty of using ChatGPT for idea generation is its ability to act as a springboard for creativity. It encourages users to think bigger, explore uncharted territories, and question the status quo. Each interaction with ChatGPT is an opportunity to venture beyond conventional thinking and discover new horizons of possibility.

Problem-Solving with ChatGPT

ChatGPT's strength is the chatbots ability to draw from a vast pool of knowledge, offering solutions that combine elements from different domains and disciplines. This cross-pollination of ideas often leads to solutions that are both creative and effective, addressing the root of the problem rather than just its symptoms. If you're facing a technical hurdle in a project, looking for ways to improve team dynamics, or seeking advice on personal growth, ChatGPT provides a range of perspectives that can help you find a way forward.

For entrepreneurs and business leaders, ChatGPT can be particularly valuable. It can help identify gaps in the market, suggest product improvements, and offer strategies for navigating complex business landscapes. In a world where the pace of change is relentless, having a tool that can provide quick, informed insights can be a great asset.

ChatGPT serves as a problem-solving coach in educational settings, guiding students through tackling difficult questions or projects. By breaking down complex problems into manageable parts, ChatGPT helps learners develop critical thinking and problem-solving skills. The abilities of ChatGPT mimic having a tutor on hand, ready to guide the student through the challenges that accompany learning new subjects.

ChatGPT also shines when it comes to personal challenges. It offers advice and strategies tailored to your situation, from managing time more effectively to dealing with interpersonal issues. It encourages a reflective approach to problem-solving, prompting you to consider different angles and potential outcomes.

Furthermore, ChatGPT is adept at helping with decision-making processes. Laying out the pros and cons of different options and suggesting criteria, ChatGPT helps make informed decisions that align with your goals and values. This aspect is particularly useful in fast-moving environments where decisions need to be made quickly and efficiently.

The true power of ChatGPT in problem-solving lies in its ability to act as a catalyst for innovation. Challenging assumptions and pushing the boundaries of conventional thinking, ChatGPT drives you to new possibilities and creative solutions.

ChatGPT stands as a pillar of support in the quest for solutions, offering a blend of knowledge, creativity, and insight. Navigating the complexities of the professional world or dealing with personal dilemmas, ChatGPT is a dependable partner, ready to help you solve problems with confidence and creativity. Its role as a brainstorming assistant ensures that no challenge is too big, and no problem is insurmountable.

Language Translation and Practice with ChatGPT

ChatGPT revolutionizes how we approach language learning, breaking down barriers and opening a world of communication. This dynamic tool serves as an invaluable companion for those looking to master a new language, offering instant translation services and practical exercises that enhance understanding and fluency.

One of the outstanding features of ChatGPT is its ability to provide language translations in real time. ChatGPT offers accurate translations that help bridge the gap between languages, whether you're trying to decipher a document, understand a foreign-language message, or communicate with someone who speaks a different language. This immediate access to translations empowers learners to immerse themselves in non-native languages, encouraging exploration and interaction without the fear of misunderstanding.

Beyond translations, ChatGPT is a fantastic tool for practicing language skills. It can simulate conversations, allowing learners to engage in dialogue as they would in real-life scenarios. This interactive approach improves speaking and comprehension skills and builds confidence in using the language in everyday situations. ChatGPT provides a safe space to practice and hone conversational abilities to master ordering food in a restaurant, asking for directions, or making small talk.

Additionally, ChatGPT assists with vocabulary expansion and grammar mastery. It can introduce new words and phrases, contextualize them in sentences, and explain grammatical rules clearly and understandably. Learners can ask for examples of verb conjugations, seek clarification on tricky syntax, or generate idiomatic expressions, all of which are crucial for achieving fluency.

For those working on writing skills, ChatGPT can be a helpful editor. It can suggest manuscript improvements, correct regular mistakes, and offer feedback on writing style. This feedback is instant and tailored to the learner's level, making it an effective tool for improving writing proficiency over time.

ChatGPT also supports pronunciation practice. Although it primarily operates through text, learners can input phonetic queries or use integrated speech recognition tools to practice pronunciation. ChatGPT can correct mispronunciations and offer tips on accent reduction, aiding learners in achieving clearer, more natural speech.

The use of ChatGPT in language learning extends to cultural learning as well. Understanding a language involves more than just mastering grammar and vocabulary; it requires an appreciation of the culture behind the language. ChatGPT can provide insights into cultural norms, expressions, and etiquette, enriching the learning experience and preparing learners for real-world interactions.

ChatGPT transforms language learning from a solitary endeavor into an interactive, engaging journey. It provides a comprehensive suite of tools for translation, practice, and cultural education, making it easier than ever to learn a new language. With ChatGPT, learners have a supportive, accessible, and intelligent partner in their pursuit of language mastery, opening new opportunities for communication and understanding in our increasingly connected world.

Health and Wellness with ChatGPT

For those in pursuit of healthier lifestyles, ChatGPT emerges as an innovative ally, guiding individuals toward achieving their wellness and fitness goals. This versatile tool provides personalized advice, tips, and support, making the process toward better health accessible and engaging.

ChatGPT stands at the forefront of health and wellness by offering tailored fitness plans. Recognizing that everyone's body and goals are unique, it crafts exercise routines that align with personal objectives, such as weight loss, muscle gain, or enhancement of overall fitness. These customized plans can consider individual preferences, limitations, and the equipment available, ensuring that fitness advice is practical and achievable.

Nutrition plays a critical role in wellness, and in this regard, ChatGPT shines by offering nutritional guidance. It can suggest healthy recipes based on dietary preferences and restrictions, whether you're vegetar ian or gluten-free or are aiming to reduce sugar intake. ChatGPT helps demystify nutrition, providing insights on balanced diets and calorie intake, making healthy eating simpler and more enjoyable.

Mental health is equally important in the wellness equation. ChatGPT serves as a supportive resource, offering strategies for stress management, mindfulness practices, and techniques for improving sleep quality. It can provide daily prompts for reflection and gratitude, encourage positive thinking, and offer tips for creating a calming bedtime routine, all contributing to mental and emotional well-being.

For those seeking to adopt new healthy habits or break old ones, ChatGPT is an invaluable motivator. It can help set realistic goals, track progress, and provide encouragement along the way. ChatGPT can assist you in increasing your water intake, taking regular breaks from screen time, or establishing a consistent exercise routine, making habit formation less daunting and more rewarding.

What's more, ChatGPT acts as a central hub for health and wellness information. It can answer questions about symptoms, explain medical conditions in ordinary language, provide insights into home remedies, and recommend when to seek professional care. While it doesn't replace medical advice from professionals, ChatGPT can offer preliminary guidance and peace of mind.

Accessibility to wellness advice is another area where ChatGPT excels. ChatGPT can answer questions, offer support, and keep you motivated 24/7. This accessibility ensures that help is always at hand, making it easier to stay committed to health and wellness goals.

Personalization is at the core of ChatGPT's approach to health and wellness. It recognizes that every individual is unique and needs customized advice that respects personal preferences, challenges, and goals. This personalized touch enhances the effectiveness of the advice and fosters a more meaningful connection to the wellness journey.

ChatGPT redefines how we approach health and wellness, making it more personalized, accessible, and integrated into daily life. By offering customized fitness plans, nutritional advice, mental health support, habit formation guidance, and a wealth of health information, ChatGPT empowers individuals to take control of their health journey. Its role as a digital wellness companion exemplifies how technology can help improve our well-being, proving that a healthier lifestyle is within reach for everyone. With ChatGPT by our side, embarking on a path to better health becomes not just a possibility but an exciting and achievable reality.

Entertainment with ChatGPT

ChatGPT opens a world of entertainment possibilities in the world of leisure and play by transforming how we engage with stories, games, and creative exploration. This digital companion goes beyond mere functionality to offer interactive and immersive experiences that captivate the imagination and bring joy to users of all ages.

Interactive storytelling with ChatGPT marks a thrilling evolution in the art of narrative. You are no longer a passive observer but an active participant, making choices that steer the story in new directions. Each decision leads to a unique pathway, ensuring that no two adventures are the same. This dynamic form of storytelling increases engagement and encourages you to think creatively, pondering the consequences of your choices and imagining alternative outcomes.

For gaming enthusiasts, ChatGPT is a great source of possibilities. It aids in creating text-based games where players navigate enchanting worlds, solve puzzles, and complete quests, all through conversation with ChatGPT. These games harken back to the classic days of interactive fiction while incorporating modern AI capabilities, offering a blend of nostalgia and innovation that appeals to seasoned gamers and newcomers.

In addition to interactive storytelling and gaming, ChatGPT can be setup to be a muse for creative expression. It can assist in writing poems, composing music lyrics, or brainstorming ideas for artworks, providing a source of inspiration and collaboration. For anyone seeking to unlock their creative potential, ChatGPT acts as a supportive partner, offering suggestions, refining ideas, and challenging creative boundaries.

Trivia and quizzes represent another engaging facet of ChatGPT's entertainment capabilities. It can generate quizzes on a wide array of topics, from general knowledge and science to pop culture and history, making learning fun and interactive. These activities serve as a delightful pastime and an informal educational tool, enriching users' knowledge.

Moreover, ChatGPT can personalize entertainment experiences by tailoring content to the user's interests and preferences. In social settings, ChatGPT enhances human interactions through games and activities enjoyed with friends and family. It can orchestrate virtual scavenger hunts, role-playing scenarios, or group storytelling sessions, fostering connection and creating memorable experiences, even when participants are miles apart.

The fusion of entertainment and technology through ChatGPT showcases the limitless potential of AI in enriching our leisure time. It offers a glimpse into a future where entertainment is not only about consumption but also about interaction, creativity, and personalization. With ChatGPT, entertainment becomes an active and dynamic experience, opening new avenues for exploration, creativity, and joy.

Case Studies of Successful ChatGPT Implementations in Personal Contexts

In the world of artificial intelligence, ChatGPT has emerged as a versatile tool for businesses and individual users seeking to transform their daily routine. These case studies look into various real-life scenarios where ChatGPT was successfully implemented, showcasing its ability to bring about tangible improvements in personal contexts, such as time saving, enhanced learning, and creative solutions.

Case Study 1: Streamlined Learning for a University Student

Sarah, a university student majoring in environmental science, faced the challenge of conducting extensive research alongside her coursework. Juggling multiple papers and assignments, she turned to ChatGPT for assistance. ChatGPT became an invaluable resource for her, aiding in gathering and summarizing information on various topics, from climate change to renewable energy sources.

The AI tool proved particularly useful in breaking down complex scientific papers into understandable summaries, saving Sarah hours of reading time. It also assisted her in brainstorming ideas for her thesis, providing insights and perspectives she hadn't considered. With ChatGPT, Sarah managed her workload more efficiently, improved her understanding of the subject matter, and enhanced the quality of her academic work.

Case Study 2: Creative Companion for A Home Chef

David, a home chef, found a creative partner in ChatGPT. His passion for cooking was sometimes hindered by his busy schedule and the dilemma of what to cook. Using ChatGPT, he started exploring new recipes and cooking styles. He input into ChatGPT the ingredients he had at hand, and ChatGPT suggested creative, easy-to-follow recipes.

This saved him time, and it introduced him to a variety of culinary techniques and cuisines. ChatGPT's ability to tailor recipes based on his dietary preferences and available ingredients transformed his cooking experience, making meal preparation more enjoyable and a less routine task.

Case Study 3: Enhanced Creative Writing

Emma, an aspiring writer, often struggled with writer's block and sought fresh ideas for her stories. She started using ChatGPT as a brainstorming tool to overcome her creative hurdles. ChatGPT helped her generate plot ideas and develop characters and suggested dialogues for her stories.

This interaction with ChatGPT provided a constant flow of ideas and helped refine her writing skills. The AI tool's suggestions ignited her creativity, enabling her to complete several short stories and a novel manuscript.

Case Study 4: Mastery of a New Language

Carlos, aiming to become fluent in French, incorporated ChatGPT into his language-learning routine. He used the tool to practice conversations, improve his grammar, and build his vocabulary. ChatGPT, with its ability to converse in multiple languages, was an excellent practice partner, offering immediate feedback and correction.

This interactive way of learning made the process more engaging for Carlos. His proficiency in French improved significantly, and he practiced daily in a stress-free environment, honing his conversational skills and confidence in using the language.

Case Study 5: Attainment of Personal Fitness Goals

Alisha, working on her fitness goals, found a coach in ChatGPT. She used the tool to plan her workout routines, seek advice on healthy eating, and stay motivated. ChatGPT provided her with personalized exercise plans while considering her fitness level and goals.

It also suggested nutritious meal plans and recipes, contributing to her overall wellness journey. The convenience and customized guidance that ChatGPT offered made it easier for Alisha to stick to her fitness regime and achieve her health objectives.

These case studies highlight the diverse and impactful ways ChatGPT can be integrated into personal lives. From aiding academic pursuits, enhancing culinary skills, boosting writing creativity, supporting language learning to helping to attain fitness goals, ChatGPT has proven to be more than just an AI tool – it's a personal assistant, a creative partner, and a learning companion.

ChatGPT is also a gateway to enhanced personal experiences. Its ease of use and powerful capabilities make it an accessible and invaluable resource for anyone looking to improve themselves. For enhanced learning, creativity, or simplification of routine tasks, ChatGPT is ready to assist.

Investigate ChatGPT's myriad applications in your life and discover how it can transform your everyday experiences. Embrace the opportunity to increase your efficiency, unleash your creativity, and enjoy a more balanced and enjoyable life with ChatGPT as your companion. The future of personal productivity and fulfillment is here, and it's yours to seize with ChatGPT.

Chapter Four

Small Business Success with ChatGPT

The rise of AI technology marks a significant shift in how small businesses operate, offering unprecedented opportunities for growth and efficiency. ChatGPT is a cutting-edge tool that empowers small enterprises to compete in today's quick-moving market. This ability opens a new world of possibilities for small business owners, from automating customer service to creating engaging marketing content.

Small businesses with their limited resources stand to gain immensely from ChatGPT. Traditional challenges like managing customer inquiries, handling repetitive tasks, and engaging with the audience on social media can now be addressed more effectively and at a fraction of the cost. ChatGPT's versatility means it can adapt to various roles within the business, streamlining operations and freeing up valuable time for entrepreneurs to focus on strategic growth.

In this chapter, we will look into the transformative potential of ChatGPT across three key areas: enhancing customer experience, streamlining business operations, and revolutionizing marketing and sales strategies. Through case studies, we'll showcase how small businesses have successfully harnessed ChatGPT to solve everyday challenges and carve out new opportunities for engagement and growth. By the end of this chapter, you will understand how to leverage ChatGPT to elevate your small business, making it more efficient, responsive, and competitive in today's market.

Seizing Opportunities with ChatGPT

ChatGPT has emerged as the solution for businesses that understand they need assistance in keeping pace with competitors in a world where technology shifts daily. For small businesses, this technology is a must-have. It levels the playing field, allowing smaller entities to punch above their weight. Think about it: customer service that never sleeps, marketing content that resonates and engages, and operations streamlined to perfection—all without the need to hire more staff or stretch resources thin. This is the promise of ChatGPT: bringing big dreams within reach for small businesses everywhere.

Adopting ChatGPT means more than just keeping up with the times; it's about seizing opportunities to innovate, stand out, and grow. It's about understanding that in today's competitive landscape, efficiency and responsiveness aren't just goals; they're necessities. ChatGPT offers a path to achieving these necessities, transforming challenges into stepping stones toward success.

Enhancing Customer Experience with ChatGPT

In today's fast-paced world, outstanding businesses offer exceptional customer service and engagement. This is where ChatGPT shines, transforming how small businesses interact with their customers. By integrating ChatGPT into their operations, businesses can now offer round-the-clock customer support, provide personalized recommendations, and instantly answer FAQs without overwhelming their human staff.

ChatGPT is there when a customer visits your website at midnight, eager to learn more about your products or needing help with an order. This level of responsiveness improves customer satisfaction and builds trust and loyalty.

In addition to answering queries, ChatGPT can take customer interaction to a new level by generating personalized recommendations for customers. It can analyze previous customer interactions and preferences to suggest products or services tailored to each customer. This personalized touch can significantly enhance the shopping experience, making customers feel understood and valued.

Moreover, ChatGPT can handle a multitude of questions simultaneously, from the uncomplicated to the complex. If it's a query about your return policy, store hours, or product specifics, ChatGPT provides accurate, automated responses. This efficiency ensures that customers get the information they need without delays, reducing frustration and improving their overall experience with your brand.

ChatGPT is revolutionizing customer service and engagement for small businesses. It offers a cost-effective way to provide exceptional, personalized customer support, ensuring that every interaction with your business is positive.

Streamlining Operations with ChatGPT

At the heart of every small business, operational efficiency is the key to growth and sustainability. ChatGPT has emerged as a powerful tool for enhancing operational efficiency by automating routine tasks that often consume precious hours and resources. This technology simplifies complex processes, from scheduling to order management, and handles basic human resources tasks, thereby unlocking new levels of productivity and cost efficiency.

Consider the tedious task of scheduling. ChatGPT can automate appointment bookings, meeting scheduling, and staff schedules with ease. It interacts with customers directly, finding suitable times for appointments and entering them into your calendar, eliminating double bookings and the back-and-forth usually required to pin down meeting times. This saves time and boosts customer experience by making their interactions with your business smooth and hassle-free.

In the realm of order management, ChatGPT revolutionizes how small businesses track and fulfill customer orders. It can automatically update inventory, process orders, and interact with customers to confirm details or provide shipping updates. This level of automation reduces the chance of human error, ensuring that operations run smoothly, and customers remain informed and satisfied.

Furthermore, ChatGPT can undertake basic human resources tasks, such as answering FAQs about company policies, onboarding new employees, and gathering feedback from staff. This frees up the human resources department to focus on more strategic tasks, like employee engagement and development, rather than getting bogged down by routine inquiries.

By integrating ChatGPT into their operations, small businesses can achieve remarkable time and cost savings. Automation of mundane tasks allows owners and employees to focus on what truly matters—growing the business and enhancing customer service. In this way, ChatGPT is a tool and a transformational force for small businesses, streamlining operations to pave the way for innovation and success.

Applications of ChatGPT for Your Small Business

In the bustling digital age in which content is king, small businesses often struggle to keep up with the demand for fresh, engaging marketing material. ChatGPT is designed to ease this burden by assisting in creating marketing content, from social media posts to email newsletters and blog articles. ChatGPT accelerates content production and ensures that the output resonates with your audience, engaging them in meaningful ways.

Marketing and Content Creation

The digital marketing landscape is vast, with content serving as the cornerstone of effective strategies. Small businesses, however, face the dual challenge of generating captivating content while managing the myriad other responsibilities that running a business entails. ChatGPT has emerged as a vital tool in this endeavor, offering the power to produce varied and compelling content that speaks directly to your audience.

For social media, where the appetite for fresh, authentic posts is insatiable, ChatGPT can be vital to success. It can generate ideas, draft posts, and suggest engaging responses to comments, helping maintain an active, vibrant presence online. This constant stream of quality content helps businesses stay at top of mind with their audience, fostering a sense of community and engagement.

Emailed newsletters, another critical touchpoint with customers, can benefit from ChatGPT's capabilities. By analyzing data on customer preferences and behaviors, ChatGPT can help personalize newsletter content, making each issue appear to be tailor-made to customers' interests. This personalization increases email open rates and engagement, driving closer connections with your audience and, ultimately, supporting customer retention and sales.

Blogging, too, becomes more manageable with ChatGPT. Generating blog content that is informative, entertaining, and relevant can be time-consuming. ChatGPT assists by suggesting topics, outlining posts, or even drafting entire articles, all in a fraction of the time it would take a human writer. This efficiency does not come at the expense of quality; ChatGPT ensures the content is engaging and tailored to your audience's interests and needs.

The beauty of ChatGPT is its versatility and adaptability. It can produce a wide range of content types, from informative pieces that establish your business as a thought leader in your industry to light-hearted posts that humanize your brand. Moreover, ChatGPT can adapt its writing style to match your brand's voice, ensuring consistency across all your marketing materials.

Sales and Lead Generation with ChatGPT

In the dynamic arena of sales, finding and nurturing potential leads is the keystone for growth. ChatGPT revolutionizes this process, offering small businesses a powerful tool to identify and engage with prospective customers more effectively than ever before. Through its advanced capabilities, ChatGPT can facilitate the initiation of sales conversations and the qualification of leads, streamlining the sales funnel and driving business success.

At its core, ChatGPT excels in understanding and generating human-like text, making it an ideal candidate for interacting with potential leads. By integrating ChatGPT into your digital platforms, your business can instantly engage visitors, answer their queries, provide information, and guide them through your offerings. This immediate interaction enhances the user experience and captures the interest of potential leads at a crucial moment in their decision-making process.

Moreover, ChatGPT can analyze the conversations to identify high-quality leads based on predefined criteria, such as interest level, budget, and readiness to purchase. This intelligent screening saves valuable time by focusing efforts on those most likely to convert, thereby increasing the efficiency of your sales strategy.

Beyond initial engagement, ChatGPT's role in lead qualification through interactive chats cannot be overstated. By asking targeted questions, it gathers essential information about the prospects, such as their needs, preferences, and pain points. This data enables a more personalized follow-up, significantly improving the chances of converting leads into customers.

Customer Feedback and Insights with ChatGPT

In the competitive landscape of business, understanding and responding to customer feedback is paramount for success. ChatGPT stands as a transformative tool in this endeavor, enabling businesses to gather and analyze customer feedback with unprecedented ease and efficiency. By leveraging ChatGPT's advanced NLP capabilities, businesses can automate feedback across various channels, ensuring a comprehensive understanding of customer sentiment.

ChatGPT can engage with customers post-interaction, soliciting feedback on products, services, and overall experience. This proactive approach ensures a steady stream of insights, providing businesses with the raw data needed to pinpoint areas for improvement. Furthermore, ChatGPT's ability to analyze text allows it to sift through feedback, identifying regular themes, trends, and specific customer concerns. This analysis is invaluable, offering businesses a clear direction on where to focus their development efforts for maximum impact.

Armed with these insights, businesses can refine their offerings to better meet customer needs. Product features can be tweaked, service protocols adjusted, and customer experience revolutionized, all based on direct feedback from the market. This iterative process of improvement, fueled by customer insights, ensures that businesses remain aligned with their audience's evolving preferences, keeping them competitive and relevant.

Additionally, using ChatGPT to analyze customer feedback can highlight strengths and areas of excellence within a business' offerings. These insights provide a foundation for building on what works well, reinforcing positive customer experiences, and ensuring that businesses continue to deliver value that resonates with their audience.

Case Studies of Successful ChatGPT Implementations in Small Business Contexts

Case Study 1: Elevating Customer Service with ChatGPT

In the bustling city center, a small, popular local bakery, Sweet Delights, faced a growing challenge. With an increasing customer base, managing inquiries, orders, and feedback through their digital channels became overwhelming. The team struggled to respond promptly, leading to missed opportunities and customer dissatisfaction. The need for an efficient, scalable solution was clear.

The bakery subsequently integrated ChatGPT into their customer service operations to automate responses to common inquiries, take orders, and gather feedback efficiently. The implementation was straightforward, thanks to ChatGPT's flexibility and ease of integration with existing platforms.

The results were transformative. Able to understand and generate human-like responses, ChatGPT took over the routine task of answering FAQs about menu items, opening hours, and reservation policies. It also handled more complex interactions, such as taking custom cake orders and offering recommendations based on customer preferences.

This shift had a profound impact on Sweet Delights' operations. The staff, previously bogged down by the volume of digital inquiries, could now focus on what they did best: creating delicious baked goods and enhancing in-store customer experiences. The bakery saw a noticeable improvement in response times to customer inquiries, leading to increased satisfaction rates. Moreover, the ability to process orders outside of business hours significantly boosted sales, turning casual website visitors into loyal customers.

The feedback collection process, also powered by ChatGPT, provided valuable insights into customer preferences and areas for improvement. This data-driven approach allowed Sweet Delights to refine its offerings and introduce new products that resonated with its audience, further driving customer loyalty and business growth.

Sweet Delights' experience with ChatGPT highlights the power of AI in transforming small business operations. The bakery enhanced its operational efficiency and elevated customer experience by addressing their customer service challenges. By doing so, they set a new standard for service excellence in the local market.

Case Study 2: Transforming Marketing with ChatGPT

In the heart of a bustling startup ecosystem, a small tech company, InnovateTech, was on the brink of a breakthrough. With a product ready to hit the market, the challenge was not in creation but communication. How could they cut through the noise and connect with their audience? The answer lay in leveraging ChatGPT for their content creation and marketing efforts.

InnovateTech's strategy was clear: utilize ChatGPT to generate engaging, informative content that highlighted the unique features and benefits of their product. They aimed to create a mix of blog posts, social media content, and email newsletters that informed and intrigued their target audience.

The implementation began with training ChatGPT on their product's specifics, target audience, and brand voice. This preparation ensured that AI could produce accurate content that resonated with InnovateTech's values and messaging. The team then set ChatGPT to work, creating a content calendar filled with topics ranging from detailed product explanations to industry trends and how InnovateTech positioned itself within the tech landscape.

The outcomes were remarkable. ChatGPT's ability to quickly churn out high-quality content meant InnovateTech could maintain a constant online presence. Blog posts written by ChatGPT attracted significant traffic to their website, with readers spending more time on pages and engaging with the material. Social media posts saw higher engagement rates, with increased shares and comments, expanding InnovateTech's reach far beyond its initial audience. Email newsletters had higher open rates and click-through rates, driving more traffic to their latest blog posts and product pages.

Most importantly, this surge in content-driven engagement translated into tangible business results. InnovateTech reported a significant uptick in inquiries about their product, leading to a noticeable increase in sales. The feedback from customers was overwhelmingly positive, with many citing the clarity and helpfulness of the content as key factors in their decision to purchase.

InnovateTech's experience with ChatGPT showcases the immense potential of AI in crafting a compelling marketing narrative. By harnessing ChatGPT's capabilities, they told their story in a way that captivated and converted.

Key Takeaways: Unleashing the Power of ChatGPT for Small Businesses

Streamlining operations. ChatGPT automates routine tasks such as scheduling, order management, and basic human resources functions. This automation significantly saves time and lowers costs, allowing business owners and their teams to focus on strategic activities that drive growth.

Enhancing customer experience. By integrating ChatGPT into customer service operations, businesses can offer 24/7 assistance, promptly respond to inquiries, and personalize customer interactions. This level of responsiveness and personalization boosts customer satisfaction and builds loyalty.

Revolutionizing marketing and content creation. ChatGPT's ability to generate engaging and relevant content rapidly transforms marketing strategies. From social media posts to email newsletters and blog articles, ChatGPT helps maintain a consistent and captivating online presence, increasing engagement and attracting potential customers.

Sales and lead generation. ChatGPT aids in identifying potential leads and initiating sales conversations. Through interactive chats, it qualifies leads, allowing businesses to concentrate their efforts on prospects most likely to convert, optimizing the sales process.

Gathering customer feedback and insights. Utilizing ChatGPT for feedback collection and analysis offers businesses critical insights into customer preferences and behavior. These insights inform product development, service improvements, and overall customer experience strategies, driving sustained business improvement.

ChatGPT represents a significant opportunity for small businesses to leverage AI for upgraded efficiency, customer satisfaction, and growth. By exploring and implementing ChatGPT in various aspects of operations, small business owners can unlock new potential and pave the way for a future marked by success and innovation.

Chapter Five

Prompt Engineering

The art of crafting prompts is a cornerstone in the dialogue between humans and AI. Prompt engineering is the practice of designing inputs for AI tools that will produce optimal outputs. The magic in getting ChatGPT to produce exactly what we need comes down to how we ask our questions or set our tasks. Prompt engineering is not about throwing words into a digital void and hoping for the best; it is a carefully honed skill akin to tuning a musical instrument to produce the perfect note.

Every interaction with ChatGPT, from the simplest query to the most complex command, hinges on the prompts we provide. These few words or sentences are the keys that unlock the vast capabilities of AI, directing its computational power and knowledge toward our specific needs.

As we move through this chapter, we will uncover the components of an effective prompt. We'll examine the elements that make prompts clear and specific, and we will delve into the importance of each word and its impact on ChatGPT's response. We'll then blend these elements into a formula for crafting prompts that hit the mark every time, enhancing the quality of our interactions with ChatGPT. Along the way, we'll also identify the common pitfalls that can derail our efforts, learning how to sidestep these traps to maintain the clarity and effectiveness of our prompts.

This exploration is not purely academic; it's a practical guide to elevate our daily interactions with ChatGPT from the mundane to the extraordinary. By mastering the art of prompt engineering, we can unlock new levels of efficiency, creativity, and insight, transforming our relationship with technology. Let's begin our exploration and discover how the right prompts can open doors to a world of possibilities.

This chapter embarks on a journey through the nuances of prompt engineering. We start by acknowledging the significance of crafting clear and specific prompts and setting the stage for successful ChatGPT interactions. From there, we dissect the elements that constitute an effective prompt, offering a blueprint for communication that ensures our intentions are perfectly understood. We then piece together these elements into a comprehensive formula designed to enhance our daily engagements with ChatGPT.

We will also examine strategies to maximize the outcomes of our well-crafted prompts, ensuring every interaction is as fruitful as possible. Finally, we navigate through regular pitfalls, learning to avoid the traps that can obscure our prompts or lead us astray. Throughout the chapter, practical tips and real-world examples illuminate the path, bridging theory with practice to equip you with the skills to refine your prompt crafting prowess.

Importance of Crafting Clear and Specific Prompts

The prompts we craft are the lead steps in guiding ChatGPT, shaping its responses and ensuring that the outcomes are as expected. At the core of this interaction is the need for clarity and specificity. The clearer and more specific a prompt, the more directly it speaks to ChatGPT, guiding it through the vastness of its data and algorithms to produce the exact response needed.

Consider a prompt as a flashlight in a dark room. The broader and more diffuse the light, the less clear the objects in the room appear. But when the light is focused and sharp, every detail of objects on which that beam shines becomes visible, allowing for precise navigation. Similarly, when prompts are vague or overly broad, the responses from ChatGPT can be equally unfocused, missing the mark on what was truly requested.

The importance of crafting clear and specific prompts cannot be overstated. Each word in a prompt acts as a directive, nudging ChatGPT toward the intended goal. The specificity of these words eliminates ambiguity, leaving no room for misinterpretation. This precision is particularly crucial in fields where the stakes are high, such as medicine, law, or safety-critical systems. In these areas, the quality of ChatGPT's response can have real-world impacts, affecting decisions, outcomes, and lives.

Moreover, the efficiency gained through well-crafted prompts is a boon for productivity. Time spent refining a prompt is an investment, paying dividends in accurate and useful ChatGPT responses on the first try. This efficiency is not solely about speed; it's about the quality of the interaction and the satisfaction derived from achieving the desired outcome with minimal friction. In the professional realm, where time is a precious commodity, quickly generating accurate reports, analyses, or creative content can be a game-changer.

But the art of prompt crafting extends beyond the professional. In everyday interactions with AI, from search engines to personal assistants, clear and specific prompts elevate the user experience, making technology more accessible and enjoyable for everyone. If you're asking for directions, seeking advice on a personal project, or querying a database; the rule is this: the clearer the prompt, the more relevant it is.

In essence, prompt engineering is a fundamental skill in the digital age, akin to the ability to ask the right question in a conversation. It's about knowing what to ask and how to ask it. This skill enhances our interactions with ChatGPT, converting them from mere transactions to meaningful exchanges. The precision of our prompts reflects the precision of our thoughts and intentions, bridging the gap between human curiosity and technological capability.

The difference a word makes can be striking. Consider two instances in the field of customer service automation. In the first case, a company used a generic prompt for its AI-powered chatbot: "Help with product." ChatGPT, lacking specific direction, often responded to customers with broad, unhelpful links to general support pages. Customers found themselves in loops, asking follow-up questions or abandoning the chat in frustration.

Contrast this with a second company that refined its ChatGPT prompt to: "Provide troubleshooting steps for [specific product] issue [detailed problem description]." ChatGPT, now armed with clarity, fetched precise solutions from its knowledge base, significantly improving customer satisfaction. The first case left users grappling with ambiguity, while the second guided them to swift resolutions.

In another example, a research team sought insights from ChatGPT for data analysis. An initial prompt, "Analyze sales data," returned a basic overview of sales figures. Realizing the need for depth, the team rephrased their prompt to "Analyze sales data for product X in region Y during Q1, highlighting trends, anomalies, and prediction for

Q2." The detailed prompt led to a comprehensive analysis, uncovering actionable insights instrumental in strategic planning.

This precision eliminates the frustration of sifting through irrelevant information, thereby enhancing user experience and trust in ChatGPT. Furthermore, reducing follow-up prompts translates into efficiency gains, conserving valuable resources for individuals and organizations.

Identifying Objectives to Be Met by Prompts

Crafting the perfect prompt is an art form, a delicate balance between saying just enough and saying it just right. The foundation of this art is understanding your objective. Before you write a single word of a prompt, it is paramount that you have clarity on what you seek to achieve with that prompt. The objective of the prompt must be crystal clear in your mind. This objective could be to gather information, trigger an action, or solicit a creative output. This clarity of purpose is the compass that guides the construction of the prompt, ensuring every element added serves its purpose toward the desired destination.

With the objective set, the process begins by laying down the path, brick by brick, with the essential elements of clarity, conciseness, context, and a call to action.

Elements of an Effective Prompt

Clarity and conciseness in prompt design are not just steps; they are the ground on which the ChatGPT dance unfolds. They ensure that each movement and request leads precisely to the desired destination without missteps.

Clarity is what guides this journey. It's about ensuring the prompt shines a clear light, removing any doubt as to what is needed from

ChatGPT. When a prompt is clear, it speaks directly to ChatGPT in a language devoid of ambiguity. A clear prompt ensures the system grasps the essence of the request, leading to responses that fit the user's actual needs. It's the difference between asking for "weather updates" and specifying "today's rainfall forecast in Paris." The latter leaves no room for error, directing ChatGPT to provide exactly what is sought.

Conciseness complements clarity by trimming the fat, leaving only the meat of the prompt. It's an exercise in efficiency, stripping away the unnecessary so the essential can shine. Conciseness is about finding that sweet spot where every word serves a purpose, and nothing is left to distract or confuse ChatGPT. This brevity is crucial; it prevents ChatGPT from getting lost in a forest of words, allowing it to focus on the core request. For example, visualize asking a friend to recommend a book for you to read. You wouldn't explain a lengthy backstory about every book you've ever liked or disliked; you'd mention the specific genre or author you're interested in. Similarly, a concise prompt directs ChatGPT's computational power exactly where it needs to be, without detours, ensuring a swift and accurate response.

The synergy of clarity and conciseness in prompt crafting cannot be overstated. Together, they form the backbone of effective communication with ChatGPT. It's a balance that ensures each request is precisely understood and acted upon.

Context and Call to Action in Prompt Crafting

A clear call to action tells ChatGPT what we want to know and how we want the information presented. Without this direction, ChatGPT may understand the request but remain uncertain about the desired action. A prompt such as "schedule a meeting" becomes exponentially more effective when transformed into "schedule a team meeting for Thursday at 10 a.m. via Zoom." This clarity in command propels ChatGPT into action, equipped with precise instructions on what to do.

Prompt context and a call to action are the twin engines that power effective prompts. They ensure that each request made to ChatGPT is heard and understood. In crafting prompts that weave together the richness of context with the clarity of a call to action, you unlock the true potential of ChatGPT as a partner in achieving your goals, making every interaction more meaningful and productive.

Incorporating New Technology into Prompt Design

Incorporating new research findings into prompt engineering is another way to maximize results. The field of AI evolves rapidly, with continuous breakthroughs offering fresh insights into how machines understand and process human language. Staying abreast of these developments and integrating them into prompt design can significantly boost the prompts' effectiveness. This could involve, for example, adapting prompts to align with new NLP models or employing cutting-edge linguistics frameworks that offer improved ChatGPT comprehension and response accuracy.

Such advanced techniques can enrich the prompt crafting toolkit, offering more nuanced and effective ways to communicate with ChatGPT. They represent the cutting edge of engaging with technology, where ongoing learning and adaptation forge the path to more meaningful and productive interactions.

Practicing Prompt Crafting

Practicing prompt generation is very important as well. It enables us to hear ChatGPT's voice, understand its interpretation of our cues, and adjust our script accordingly. Through this iterative process, prompts are refined and sharpened into tools that carve out precise and meaningful responses.

Chapter Six

The Boundaries of ChatGPT (2024)

The landscape of artificial intelligence (AI) has undergone a dramatic transformation over the past few years, with ChatGPT at the forefront of this shift. This remarkable tool has opened new avenues for creativity, productivity, and interaction. However, it's crucial to acknowledge that ChatGPT, like any technology, has its limitations. Understanding these boundaries is the key to harnessing its full potential and integrating it seamlessly into your personal life and work processes. This chapter will demystify ChatGPT's limits as they currently stand in 2024. It will set realistic expectations and guide you in navigating these constraints to make the most of this powerful tool.

Realistic Expectations for ChatGPT Performance

Accuracy and reliability are paramount when assessing ChatGPT's output. While often impressive, the information provided by ChatGPT may not always be accurate and up to date, necessitating a critical evaluation of its responses. Recognizing the conditions under which ChatGPT performs best can significantly improve user experience and outcome reliability.

The tool's creativity and innovation are groundbreaking, yet they have their boundaries. ChatGPT can generate novel ideas and solutions, but its suggestions are ultimately based on patterns in the data it is trained on. This means the originality and applicability of its ideas may not always meet user expectations, especially for tasks requiring out-of-the-box thinking.

ChatGPT is designed to mimic human conversational abilities, including empathy and humor, to a certain extent. However, its responses can sometimes miss the mark in understanding the nuances of human emotion or cultural context, impacting the quality of engagement. For this reason, users should strive to maintain realistic expectations for ChatGPT's performance.

Technical Limitations and Constraints of ChatGPT (2024)

As we navigate the capabilities of ChatGPT in 2024, understanding its technical limitations is crucial for harnessing its power effectively. This exploration sheds light on the computational and algorithmic boundaries that shape the experiences and outcomes of using ChatGPT.

At its core, ChatGPT operates within a complex web of algorithms and computational processes. These drive its ability to understand and generate human-like text. However, these engines are not limitless. They require substantial computational resources, including processing power and memory, which are not infinite. For instance, when ChatGPT attempts to generate responses to particularly complex queries or engage in lengthy conversations, it may encounter the boundaries of its computational capabilities. This can lead to slower response times or limitations in the depth and complexity of its outputs.

From an ethical and societal perspective, using ChatGPT raises questions about privacy, data security, and the ethical implications of AI-generated content. Legal and ethical guidelines shape how ChatGPT can be applied, particularly in sensitive areas like personal advice or content creation that may have copyright implications. These concerns are vital to consider, as they influence the trustworthiness and applicability of ChatGPT in various domains.

Furthermore, the algorithms that power ChatGPT are designed based on patterns in the data they train on, such as keywords and language nuances. While this enables the AI to produce remarkably coherent and contextually relevant responses, it also binds it to the confines of its training data. This means there are areas where ChatGPT may struggle, such as understanding highly specialized or new topics that were not well-represented in its training set. The AI's ability to grasp and generate content in these areas can be limited, reflecting the gap between the vastness of human knowledge and the dataset it has access to.

Moreover, the nature of these algorithms dictates that ChatGPT's understanding of context and nuance is not always perfect. While there have been advancements in NLP, the subtleties of human communication can sometimes elude ChatGPT. These imperfections include interpreting the tone, emotional cues, or cultural nuances embedded in a conversation. The AI's responses, while intelligent, may not always capture the full depth of human expression or the intricacies of specific contexts.

These technical limitations highlight the importance of recognizing ChatGPT as a remarkably advanced tool. It operates within a framework defined by current technological capabilities and the boundaries of its programming. As users, our understanding of these constraints is the key to maximizing the benefits of ChatGPT, allowing us to navigate its limitations while appreciating the vast potential. This knowledge equips us to employ ChatGPT more effectively, leveraging its strengths to complement our interactions with technology while remaining mindful of the areas where human insight and expertise remain indispensable.

Data and Knowledge Boundaries

ChatGPT operates within certain bounds, particularly with data and knowledge. One of the most defining aspects of these limitations is the cutoff date of the knowledge used to generate responses to prompts. ChatGPT's understanding and responses are based on the information available up to a specific point in time, beyond which it lacks awareness of new developments, events, or discoveries.

This cutoff date is significant because it delineates the horizon of ChatGPT's world. Imagine asking ChatGPT about the latest advancements in space exploration or the outcomes of recent global events. If these occur after its last update, ChatGPT won't be able to provide accurate or current information.

Furthermore, ChatGPT's grasp of context and real-time information faces challenges. While it can generate responses based on historical data and pre-existing knowledge, interpreting the nuances of a rapidly changing situation or the specific context of a live event is beyond its reach. For example, in responding to queries about stock market trends or breaking news, ChatGPT may offer general principles or historical data but cannot provide minute-by-minute updates or the immediate implications of a just-occurring event.

These boundaries underscore the importance of using ChatGPT with an awareness of its temporal and contextual constraints. While it is a powerful tool for generating insights, answering questions, and stimulating ideas based on a vast repository of pre-existing information, its utility as a source of the latest news or developments is limited. Recognizing these limitations helps users navigate ChatGPT more effectively, leveraging its strengths in areas where it excels while seeking real-time sources and human expertise for the latest information and analysis.

Legal concerns are paramount, as the deployment of ChatGPT intersects with copyright laws, data protection regulations, and other legal frameworks designed to safeguard intellectual property and personal information. For instance, when ChatGPT generates content, questions about the originality and ownership of this AI-created material may arise, challenging existing copyright laws that were not designed with AI in mind.

Ethical considerations also play a critical role, especially regarding transparency and accountability. The use of ChatGPT in creating news articles, academic papers, or other forms of content without clear disclosure that it is AI-generated raises ethical questions. It blurs the lines between human and machine creativity, potentially misleading audiences and eroding trust in digital content.

Privacy concerns are equally significant. ChatGPT, through its interactions, collects vast amounts of data from users. This raises questions about how this data is stored, used, and protected. With regulations like the General Data Protection Regulation (GDPR) in Europe, ensuring compliance while leveraging AI technologies like ChatGPT requires careful navigation to protect users' privacy and prevent misuse of personal information.

These ethical and societal constraints highlight the need for a balanced approach to integrating ChatGPT into various facets of life and work. They underscore the importance of developing and adhering to robust ethical guidelines and legal frameworks that ensure the technology is used in ways that are responsible, transparent, and respectful of individual rights and societal values. As we move forward, these considerations will remain at the forefront of discussions on the future of AI and its place in society. They will guide the development and application of these technologies in a manner that aligns with our collective values and norms.

Creativity and Innovation Limits

ChatGPT's ability to generate new content, from writing poems to proposing solutions for theoretical problems, showcases its creative prowess. It can uniquely combine elements from its extensive training data, often leading to innovative and insightful outputs. Yet, the boundaries of ChatGPT's creativity are defined by the data it was educated from. Its so-called "creativity" is not derived from consciousness or personal experience but from algorithms processing existing human-created content.

This distinction between algorithms and consciousness is crucial when evaluating ChatGPT's problem-solving capabilities. While it can offer a range of solutions or creative outputs, these are ultimately reconstructions or new combinations of what it has learned. For challenges requiring outside-the-box thinking or a deep understanding of human emotions and experiences, ChatGPT's solutions may not always capture the full range of human creativity or the subtlety of innovative thought. Recognizing these limitations allows users to leverage ChatGPT effectively within its capabilities, using it as a brainstorming tool or a starting point for creative exploration while turning to human intuition and creativity for tasks that require a more profound, empathetic touch.

Setting realistic expectations for ChatGPT's performance is essential in harnessing its full potential. By understanding where it excels and acknowledging its limitations, users can effectively integrate ChatGPT into their workflow, studies, or creative processes. This balanced approach maximizes the benefits of ChatGPT, leveraging its strengths in data processing and content generation while remaining mindful of the need for human oversight and input in areas such as accuracy verification, ethical considerations, and creative innovation.

In artificial intelligence, the ability of ChatGPT to engage in conversations stands out as a testament to the strides made in technology. This capability showcases the technical prowess behind ChatGPT and opens a window into the future of human-AI interaction. As we delve into the nuances of conversational engagement, including empathy and humor, it becomes clear that setting realistic expectations is crucial for maximizing the benefits of ChatGPT across various applications.

The art of conversation involves more than just exchanging words. It's about understanding context, sensing mood, and, sometimes, reading between the lines. ChatGPT, with its vast database of language patterns and scenarios, can mimic these aspects of human interaction to a certain extent. It can generate contextually appropriate responses and infuse its replies with a sense of humor or a semblance of empathy. This ability to engage in a seemingly natural manner is one of ChatGPT's most fascinating features.

However, the essence of conversational engagement is understanding and responding to the emotional nuances, a domain where ChatGPT has limitations. While it can simulate empathy based on learned patterns, it doesn't "feel" emotions as humans do. Its humor and expressions of empathy reflect its programming and training data rather than genuine emotional responses. Recognizing this distinction is the key to setting realistic expectations for ChatGPT's conversational abilities.

It can participate in engaging discussions, provide support, and make jokes, but it does so within the confines of its programming.

This understanding is crucial when leveraging ChatGPT for tasks requiring emotional intelligence. In customer service, for example, ChatGPT can handle inquiries and provide information efficiently, but human intervention may be necessary for situations that require genuine empathy and understanding. Similarly, in therapeutic or counseling contexts, ChatGPT can offer preliminary support or general advice, but it cannot replace the nuanced understanding and personal touch of a human.

Setting realistic expectations for ChatGPT's performance in conversational engagement enables users to leverage its strengths while acknowledging its limitations. It is a powerful tool for automating responses, generating content, and entertaining users, but it operates within its design and training. Recognizing this helps effectively integrate ChatGPT into communication strategies, ensuring that it complements human efforts rather than attempting to replace the irreplaceable aspects of human interaction.

Areas where Improvements are Anticipated for the Near Future

The pace at which technology is advancing suggests ChatGPT may soon overcome its limitations. As we look ahead, several areas of technological innovation hold promise for pushing these boundaries further, enhancing ChatGPT's capabilities and addressing its current constraints.

Technological advances. The future of AI, particularly in the context of ChatGPT, is poised for significant breakthroughs. One of the most anticipated advancements is in the realm of computational power.

Quantum computing, still in its early stages, holds the potential to exponentially increase the processing capabilities available to AI systems. Quantum computing is a calculation that uses principles of fundamental physics to solve extremely complex problems that traditional digital computers cannot. This leap in computational ability would enable ChatGPT to process and analyze data at speeds unattainable with current technology, dramatically improving its response time and the complexity of tasks it can handle.

Another promising area is algorithmic efficiency. Researchers are continually developing new models and algorithms that can learn more efficiently from data while requiring less computational resources for training. These advancements could enable ChatGPT to understand and generate human language with greater accuracy and nuance. Moreover, improvements in unsupervised and semi-supervised learning models may allow ChatGPT to learn from a broader range of data sources, including real-time information, thereby expanding its knowledge base and relevance.

The development of more advanced NLP techniques is also on the horizon. These techniques aim to improve ChatGPT's ability to understand context, sarcasm, and subtleties in human communication, making its interactions more nuanced and human-like. Enhanced NLP models could enable ChatGPT to offer more accurate and contextually appropriate responses, improving its utility in complex conversational scenarios.

In addition to these technological advancements, there is a growing focus on ethical AI development. This includes creating frameworks and guidelines to ensure AI systems like ChatGPT are developed and used in ways that are ethical, transparent, and respectful of privacy and data security. As these frameworks evolve, they will address societal and ethical concerns while enhancing trust in AI technologies, facilitating their broader acceptance and integration into various aspects of life and work.

These anticipated advancements in AI technology represent a convergence of computational power, algorithmic innovation, and ethical development. Together, they promise to extend the capabilities of ChatGPT, transforming it into an even more powerful tool for individuals and businesses alike. By overcoming current limitations, these advancements will open new avenues for application and exploration, making ChatGPT an even more integral part of our digital future.

Data accessibility and quality. The future of data collection and processing shines bright with potential, promising significant leaps forward in the quality of data and ease of access. One of the main advancements is in the realm of data collection methods. Innovations like the Internet of Things (IoT) – the network of interconnected devices and the technology that enables communication between these devices and the cloud, as well as between the devices themselves – are expanding the gathered data sources, providing a richer, more diverse pool of information. This proliferation of data sources, from everyday devices to industrial sensors, means AI systems like ChatGPT will have access to a broader spectrum of real-time data, enabling them to offer insights and responses that are more accurate and contextually relevant.

Moreover, the quality of data is improving dramatically. Enhanced data cleaning and preprocessing techniques are developing, ensuring that the information fed into AI systems is of the highest fidelity. These techniques aim to reduce noise (irrelevant or meaningless data or output occurring along with desired information), eliminate irrelevant information, and highlight valuable data, thereby improving the efficiency of AI learning processes and the accuracy of their outputs.

Another significant advancement is in data processing. With more powerful computing technologies and algorithms, data processing speed and efficiency are expected to increase exponentially. AI systems will learn from and adapt to this new data in near real-time, significantly enhancing their responsiveness and versatility.

The implications of these advancements for AI systems like ChatGPT are profound. Improved data accessibility and quality will enable these systems to understand and interact with the world in more nuanced and sophisticated ways. For instance, ChatGPT could offer more timely and relevant advice, drawing on a vast and constantly updated database of information. It could also provide more accurate predictions and analyses, thanks to the improved quality of the data it relies on.

Furthermore, data collection and processing advancements are likely to make AI systems more accessible and useful across a wider range of applications. From healthcare, where real-time patient data can inform personalized treatment plans, to urban planning, where diverse datasets can help model and predict city growth, the potential is nearly limitless.

These improvements will broaden the capabilities of systems like ChatGPT and open new possibilities for their application, impacting every corner of society. With a foundation built on richer, more accessible data, the next generation of AI is poised to exceed our current expectations, driving innovation and progress in ways we have yet to imagine.

Ethical and governance frameworks. The trajectory of ChatGPT's development is closely intertwined with the evolving landscape of ethical standards and governance frameworks. These guidelines serve as a compass, directing the technology toward a future where innovation is balanced with responsibility. As we forge ahead, these frameworks are expected to become more sophisticated, addressing the nuanced challenges that have emerged with AI's integration into everyday life.

One of the most significant areas of focus is data privacy and security. With AI systems like ChatGPT relying heavily on vast datasets, ensuring the privacy and security of this data is paramount. Future regulations are likely to introduce more stringent requirements for data handling, compelling developers to adopt advanced encryption methods and secure data storage solutions.

Another critical aspect is the accountability of AI systems. As these technologies become more autonomous, establishing clear lines of accountability for their actions is essential. Upcoming ethical frameworks are expected to address this by setting standards for transparency in AI systems. By making AI's decision-making processes more transparent, users can understand and trust the outcomes generated by ChatGPT and similar technologies.

Furthermore, the issue of bias in AI is a pressing concern that future ethical guidelines are set to tackle. By mandating more diverse and representative training datasets, as well as regular auditing for bias, these frameworks will guide the development of more equitable AI systems. This will ensure that technologies like ChatGPT serve all segments of society fairly, without perpetuating existing disparities.

Understanding the current limitations and future potential of ChatGPT is essential for users looking to leverage this technology effectively. With limitations in technical capabilities, data knowledge, and ethical considerations, there's a bright future ahead with expected advancements that will likely overcome many of these challenges. By setting realistic expectations and staying informed about the evolving landscape of AI, users can effectively integrate ChatGPT into their everyday lives and businesses, leveraging its strengths while navigating its limitations.

Chapter Seven

Potential Dangers of ChatGPT and Strategies for Safe Use

The emergence of ChatGPT marks a significant milestone in the shift toward sophisticated digital communication. This advanced AI has the power to transform industries, enhance our daily interactions, and provide solutions to complex problems with unprecedented ease. However, beneath these remarkable capabilities lie ethical considerations and potential risks that demand our attention. The importance of proceeding with caution when using ChatGPT cannot be overstated, as the implications of ChatGPT's widespread use extend far beyond the technological realm, touching on the very fabric of society.

The ethical concerns associated with ChatGPT revolve around several key issues. Misinformation and disinformation represent significant challenges, as the AI's ability to generate plausible yet false content can have far-reaching consequences in an era where information is a powerful currency. Privacy and data security are also paramount, with the vast amounts of personal information processed by ChatGPT raising questions about protecting user data. Furthermore, the potential for AI to foster dependence and dehumanization cannot be ignored, as increased reliance on digital interactions may impact social connections and emotional well-being.

These ethical dilemmas compound potential biases inherent in language generation. The data ChatGPT is trained on can reflect existing prejudices, leading to responses that may inadvertently perpetuate stereotypes or amplify societal divisions. Addressing these biases requires concerted effort and innovative strategies to ensure that AI serves as a force for good, promoting inclusivity and understanding.

In response to these challenges, strategies for the responsible and safe use of ChatGPT are emerging. Education and awareness are crucial, empowering users to recognize the capabilities and limitations of AI. Ethical guidelines and best practices offer a framework for the conscientious deployment of ChatGPT across various domains. Additionally, technological safeguards, including content filters and monitoring tools, are being developed to mitigate risks and protect users.

As we navigate the complexities of integrating ChatGPT into our lives and work, the collective responsibility of developers, users, and policymakers is clear. By addressing the ethical concerns, biases, and potential dangers head-on, we can harness the power of ChatGPT responsibly, ensuring that this revolutionary technology enriches society while safeguarding against its risks. ChatGPT does have issues and complications, however, with careful consideration and collaborative effort, we can steer the course toward a future where AI is a monument of progress, guided by equity, respect, and human dignity.

Potential Dangers

Misinformation and disinformation. The distinction between misinformation, which is false information shared without harmful intent, and disinformation, deliberately crafted to deceive, is crucial. ChatGPT, by design, does not distinguish between the two, relying instead on the input it receives and the vast stores of data it has access to. This neutrality becomes a double-edged sword when the AI generates content on contentious or highly polarized topics.

A hypothetical scenario illustrates the potential impact of this challenge. Consider a situation where ChatGPT is used to generate a news article on a recent, highly politicized event. Depending on the data it has been trained on and the biases inherent in that data, the article could skew toward a particular point of view, spreading misinformation or even disinformation. The AI's credibility lends weight to the article, making it more likely for readers to accept the information as true, thereby influencing public opinion based on potentially biased or false information.

The ethical concerns extend beyond the spread of false information to the broader implications for democracy and public trust. In an era where information is power, the ability of AI, including ChatGPT, to produce content that may be indistinguishable from that created by humans poses a threat to the integrity of the information ecosystem. This is evidenced by the potential for individuals to misuse ChatGPT as they seek to manipulate public opinion or spread false information for personal or political gain.

Addressing these challenges requires a multifaceted approach. On one hand, developers and researchers are tasked with refining AI technologies to better detect and mitigate bias, ensuring the content generated by ChatGPT is as accurate and unbiased as possible. On the other hand, there is a pressing need for media literacy among the general public to empower individuals to critically evaluate the information they encounter, regardless of the source.

Furthermore, regulatory measures could play a crucial role in mitigating the risks associated with AI-generated content. Policies and frameworks designed to increase transparency around the use of AI in content creation, along with strict guidelines on the ethical use of such technologies, could help safeguard against the spread of misinformation and disinformation.

The ethical concerns surrounding ChatGPT and its potential role in spreading false information underscore the need for a balanced and cautious approach to AI development and deployment. By recognizing the challenges and actively seeking solutions, we can harness the power of AI for good, ensuring that technologies like ChatGPT contribute to the advancement of knowledge and society responsibly and ethically.

Privacy and data security breach. In the digital age, privacy and data security are critically important concerns, especially with the advent of sophisticated AI technologies like ChatGPT. These systems, designed to process and generate human-like text, rely on vast amounts of data, raising critical questions about safeguarding user information. The core issue lies in the balance between leveraging AI for its immense benefits and protecting individual privacy rights.

Collection, storage, and use of data by AI systems pose a significant risk if not managed with the utmost care. Personal information, after being fed into the AI, becomes part of a larger dataset used for training and refining the technology. Without stringent security measures, this data could fall prey to breaches, exposing sensitive user information to unauthorized parties. Moreover, the ethical use of this data by AI developers and companies comes into question, highlighting the need for clear regulations and guidelines to ensure that user data is not misused or exploited.

The concerns extend beyond the immediate privacy implications. The security of user information is fundamental to maintaining trust in AI technologies. Breaches or misuse of data could erode public confidence, hampering the adoption and success of AI. Therefore, implementing advanced encryption methods, secure data storage solutions, and transparent data policies becomes essential in addressing these challenges, ensuring that privacy and data security are upheld in the era of AI.

Dependence and dehumanization. As AI technologies become more integrated into day-to-day life, the potential for dependence and dehumanization warrants careful consideration. ChatGPT can mimic human interaction, presenting a double-edged sword. On one side, it offers unprecedented convenience and efficiency, aiding in tasks ranging from customer service to personal companionship. On the other, it risks fostering a reliance on digital communication, potentially diminishing the value placed on human contact and empathy.

This second possibility paints a picture in which conversations, once the domain of human interaction, increasingly occur between humans and machines. This shift could lead to social isolation, as individuals may prefer the simplicity and predictability of AI interactions over the complexities of human relationships. Furthermore, the constant engagement with AI could erode empathy, with the nuances of human emotion and understanding getting lost in translation to digital responses.

Combating these potential outcomes requires a balanced approach to AI integration. Encouraging AI to augment human interaction rather than replace it could mitigate the risks of dependence and dehumanization. Additionally, fostering environments that prioritize human connections and emphasizing the irreplaceable value of empathy and emotional understanding in education and community settings are crucial steps in preserving the human element in a technology-driven world.

Addressing the concerns of privacy, data security, dependence, and dehumanization in the context of AI technologies like ChatGPT is essential for navigating the future. By implementing safeguards and regulations while promoting a culture that values human connection, we can harness the benefits of AI while protecting humanity's core aspects.

Potential biases in language generation. At the heart of ChatGPT's revolutionary language generation capabilities lies its training data. While this internet-sourced data enables ChatGPT to mimic human-like conversations and provide informative responses, it also harbors the risk of source data bias. This form of bias occurs when the data used to train the AI reflects historical inequalities or prejudices, inadvertently weaving these biases into the fabric of ChatGPT's responses.

The implications of source data bias are profound, affecting not just the accuracy of information provided but also perpetuating societal biases. For instance, if ChatGPT uses data that disproportionately associates certain professions with a specific gender, its responses may echo these stereotypes, thus reinforcing outdated societal norms. Similarly, biases in training data related to race, ethnicity, or culture can lead to responses that either marginalize or misrepresent diverse groups, impacting users who rely on ChatGPT for information, education, or entertainment.

The AI community is acutely aware of the challenges posed by source data bias and is making efforts to detect and mitigate its impact. One approach involves diversifying the data sources used for training, ensuring they represent a wide spectrum of perspectives and experiences. This includes incorporating texts from different cultures, languages, and demographic groups to create a more balanced and inclusive dataset.

Additionally, techniques such as bias detection algorithms are developing to identify and correct skewed patterns in training data. These algorithms analyze the AI's responses for evidence of bias, allowing developers to adjust the training process accordingly. Another mitigation strategy is the use of external audits, where independent experts review the AI's output to identify biases, providing additional layers of scrutiny.

Efforts within the AI community to address source data bias are ongoing and critical to ensuring that technologies like ChatGPT serve all users equitably. By acknowledging the potential for bias and implementing robust detection and mitigation strategies, developers can minimize the impact of these biases, paving the way for more accurate, fair, and inclusive AI-generated content. This ongoing battle against bias in AI underscores the importance of vigilance and continuous improvement in the development and deployment of technologies that have become integral to our personal lives.

Amplification of stereotypes. The emergence of AI-generated content has brought to light a significant ethical dilemma: the risk of perpetuating stereotypes. When AI models like ChatGPT generate responses based on training data collected from the internet, they risk replicating and amplifying existing societal stereotypes. This is because the AI does not possess the ability to discern right from wrong or ethical from unethical; it merely reflects the data fed to it. For instance, if the bulk of the training data associates certain behaviors, roles, or characteristics with specific genders, ethnicities, or other demographic groups, ChatGPT may unintentionally reinforce these stereotypes in its responses.

The implications of such an outcome are far-reaching, affecting individual perceptions and shaping societal norms. When stereotypes perpetuate something as seemingly authoritative from AI, it lends unwarranted credibility to these biases, potentially influencing the beliefs and attitudes of its users. This scenario underscores the critical need for vigilance and proactive measures to prevent AI from becoming a conduit for spreading stereotypes.

Strategies for Safe Use

Mitigation strategies for safe use. Recognizing the gravity of this issue, the AI community has rallied to develop and implement strategies for reducing bias in AI models. One of the primary approaches is the careful curation and diversification of training data. By ensuring that the data reflects a broad spectrum of human experiences and perspectives, developers can minimize the model's exposure to biased or stereotypical content. This involves including diverse sources of information and actively seeking out and incorporating content that challenges prevailing stereotypes.

Another effective strategy is the implementation of bias detection algorithms. These sophisticated tools sift through AI responses, identifying patterns or responses that may indicate bias. Once detected, these biases can be addressed by adjusting the training data or fine-tuning the model's algorithms to counteract the detected biases.

In addition to these technical solutions, there is a growing emphasis on ethical oversight. This involves establishing panels or committees comprising individuals from diverse backgrounds who can review AI-generated content for bias and stereotypes. Their insights and perspectives are invaluable in identifying subtle biases that may not be apparent to developers or algorithms.

Furthermore, by openly discussing the potential for bias and the measures taken to address it, AI developers can foster trust and encourage a collaborative effort to tackle these challenges. Publicly sharing the methodologies for bias detection and mitigation also allows for external critique and suggestions, further refining the strategies employed.

The concerted effort to reduce bias in AI models like ChatGPT is a testament to the AI community's commitment to ethical technology development. Through a combination of technical innovation, ethical oversight, and transparent practices, there is a clear path forward to minimizing the amplification of stereotypes in AI-generated content, ensuring that these powerful tools serve to unite rather than divide.

Strategies for responsible and safe use of ChatGPT. In the rapidly evolving landscape of artificial intelligence, understanding the capabilities and limitations of technologies like ChatGPT is crucial for harnessing their potential responsibly. Educating users on what ChatGPT can and cannot do goes beyond merely acquainting them with a list of functions. It involves a comprehensive approach to awareness, ensuring individuals and organizations are equipped to use this powerful tool in productive and safe ways.

The first step in user education is to demystify AI technology. Simplifying the complex algorithms and processes behind ChatGPT helps users appreciate the intricacies of AI interactions. Workshops, webinars, and online courses can play a significant role in this, offering accessible platforms for learning and discussion. These educational initiatives should cover the basics of how ChatGPT operates, including an honest discussion about the sources of its training data and how this may influence its responses.

Awareness campaigns are another vital strategy, focusing on the ethical use of ChatGPT. These campaigns can highlight scenarios where reliance on AI may not be appropriate, such as sensitive emotional support roles or situations requiring critical human judgment. By outlining clear use cases and potential pitfalls, users can better navigate when and how to integrate ChatGPT into their workflows or daily routines.

Moreover, developing a set of guidelines for interacting with ChatGPT can guide users in maintaining a responsible approach. These guidelines could include recommendations on verifying information provided by ChatGPT, respecting privacy when sharing sensitive data, and understanding the importance of context in formulating queries. Additionally, emphasizing the significance of human oversight cannot be overstated. Encouraging users to evaluate AI-generated content critically and the use of ChatGPT as an aid rather than a substitute for human intellect fosters a balanced relationship with technology.

Initiatives and tools that support the safe deployment of AI technologies are also important. Platforms that offer real-time monitoring of AI interactions help identify and mitigate potential misuse. Furthermore, feedback mechanisms where users can report inaccuracies or biases in ChatGPT's responses encourage a collaborative effort toward improving the technology.

In essence, educating users about ChatGPT's capabilities and limitations is a foundational aspect of responsible AI use. Through training and awareness, integrating ChatGPT into society and various sectors can be navigated with a greater sense of security and ethical alignment. This proactive approach improves the utility of ChatGPT and safeguards the values and norms essential in a technology-driven future.

Ethical guidelines and best practices. In the digital era, AI technologies like ChatGPT will integrate into various aspects of life and work, presenting opportunities and challenges. To responsibly navigate this landscape, it's imperative to adhere to the ethical guidelines and best practices listed below, which ensure the beneficial use of ChatGPT while mitigating potential risks.

- **Transparency is fundamental.** Users should be informed when interacting with AI, distinguishing clearly between human and machine-generated content. This clarity is crucial in maintaining trust, particularly in sensitive areas such as mental health support, education, and customer service. Providing users with information about how ChatGPT operates, including its reliance on pre-existing data for responses, fosters an environment of informed usage.

- **Accuracy and verification practices are essential.** When ChatGPT generates informational content, users and organizations should cross-check AI-generated information against reliable sources before dissemination. Encouraging a culture of skepticism and verification among users can significantly reduce the spread of misinformation.

- **Privacy protection measures must be a top priority**. Users should be cautious about sharing personal or sensitive information with ChatGPT. Organizations deploying ChatGPT must ensure robust data protection measures and adherence to data privacy laws and regulations. Implementing secure data practices, such as anonymizing user interactions with ChatGPT, can safeguard user privacy.

- **Bias and fairness considerations are paramount**. Users and developers must be aware of the potential for AI to reflect and amplify societal biases. Regular audits and updates to ChatGPT's training data can help minimize these biases, promoting fairness and inclusivity. Engaging diverse groups in developing and reviewing AI applications ensures a broader perspective on potential biases.

- **Deployment must be responsible.** This involves considering the impact of ChatGPT on human jobs and societal norms. Organizations should assess the implications of automating tasks with AI, ensuring that technology augments human work without displacing it unnecessarily. Providing training opportunities for employees can facilitate a smooth transition to AI-enhanced workflows.

- **Empower users through education.** Educating users about AI's capabilities and limitations enables individuals to make informed decisions about when and how to use ChatGPT. Workshops, tutorials, and accessible resources about AI ethics and best practices can equip users with the knowledge to interact with AI technologies responsibly.

- **Engage with the community.** Ongoing dialogue about the ethical use of AI is vital. Platforms for feedback and discussion allow users to share experiences, raise concerns, and suggest improvements. This collective input can guide the evolution of ChatGPT in a direction that aligns with societal values and needs.

- **Innovation in safety measures is crucial.** Developing tools to detect and mitigate the misuse of AI, including technologies that monitor AI-generated content for harmful or unethical outputs, can play a significant role in maintaining the integrity of digital spaces.

Technological Safeguards. With artificial intelligence, ensuring the responsible and safe use of technologies like ChatGPT is crucial. As

AI continues to weave its way into the fabric of society, developing and implementing technological safeguards stand as critical measures to mitigate risks associated with its use. These safeguards, including content filters and monitoring tools, are designed to protect users from potential harm and ensure that interactions with AI remain beneficial and secure.

Content filters play a vital role in this protective framework. By setting parameters that prevent the generation of harmful or inappropriate content, these filters act as gatekeepers, ensuring the information provided by ChatGPT adheres to ethical standards and societal norms.

This is particularly important in environments where AI is accessible to younger audiences or used in educational settings. Customizable content filters block specific types of information, providing a tailored approach to safeguarding against the dissemination of false, biased, or sensitive material.

Monitoring tools complement content filters by offering real-time oversight of AI interactions. These tools analyze conversations and content generated by ChatGPT, identifying patterns or instances that may indicate misuse or the emergence of ethical concerns. Monitoring can flag issues for human review, enabling timely interventions when necessary. This continuous oversight is crucial in dynamic settings where the context and appropriateness of content can rapidly change.

The integration of technological safeguards into AI must be accompanied by transparency and control. Users should have clear information about the safeguards and the ability to adjust settings according to their preferences and needs. Transparency and control will empower individuals and organizations to use ChatGPT in a manner that aligns with their ethical guidelines and risk tolerance.

Developing these safeguards is ongoing, driven by technological advances and evolving understandings of ethical AI use. Collaboration among developers, users, and regulatory bodies is essential to refine these tools, ensuring they remain effective in the face of new challenges and opportunities presented by AI technologies.

Implementing technological safeguards such as content filters and monitoring tools is a foundational step in the responsible deployment of ChatGPT. These measures provide a safety net, enabling users to access the benefits of AI while mitigating risks. As we navigate the complexities of integrating AI into various aspects of society, the commitment to developing and maintaining robust technological safeguards will be the key to fostering a safe, ethical, and productive AI-enhanced future.

Addressing the ethical concerns, biases, and the call for safe usage of ChatGPT requires a concerted effort from all stakeholders. Developers, users, and policymakers share a collective responsibility in shaping the trajectory of AI toward a future that honors ethical principles, promotes fairness, and safeguards human dignity. Through collaboration and commitment to these principles, the vast potential of ChatGPT can be harnessed in a manner that benefits society while minimizing harm, ensuring a balanced coexistence with this transformative technology.

Chapter Eight

Examples of Prompts

Navigating the vast capabilities of ChatGPT requires not just an understanding of its potential but also the art of prompt engineering. This craft, essential for unlocking the full utility of ChatGPT, hinges on the strategic formulation of prompts to elicit the most accurate, creative, and useful responses from the AI. Prompt engineering transcends mere question-asking; it involves a nuanced approach to communication, where clarity, specificity, and intent directly influence the quality of ChatGPT's output.

Well-crafted prompts act as keys that unlock the trove of ChatGPT's knowledge and capabilities. Whether generating detailed plans, providing educational content, sparking creativity, or offering technical solutions, the effectiveness of the AI's response is significantly strengthened by the precision and thoughtfulness of the prompt. This chapter investigates prompt examples, offering a rich tapestry of scenarios where targeted prompts transform ChatGPT from a mere conversational partner to an invaluable assistant in various facets of personal life and small business operations.

Prompts for Everyday Tasks

In the dynamic world we navigate daily, the fusion of artificial intelligence with our routine tasks offers a promising horizon of efficiency and creativity. Harnessing the capabilities of ChatGPT through well-structured prompts can transform the mundane into the extraordinary, turning everyday tasks into seamless operations. The following examples are prompts that enable ChatGPT to assist with practical daily activities.

Organizing daily schedules. "Can you help me create a balanced schedule for tomorrow? I need to include eight hours of work, two hours of leisure, exercise for an hour, and family time. Please allocate time for meals and rest."

Planning meals for the week. "Based on a balanced diet, generate a meal plan for a family of four for the upcoming week. Include three meals per day and two snack options, considering a mix of vegetarian and chicken-based dishes."

Creating grocery shopping lists. "Given my meal plan for the week, what groceries do I need to buy? Please categorize the list by fruits, vegetables, proteins, dairy, and pantry staples."

Suggesting exercise routines. "I'm looking for a thirty-minute home exercise routine that doesn't require equipment. My goal is to improve strength and flexibility. Can you suggest a daily plan for beginners?"

Recommending books based on interest. "I enjoy mysteries and historical fiction. Can you recommend five books that blend these genres? Please provide a brief summary and the reason for each recommendation."

Through prompts such as these, ChatGPT can assist in navigating the complexities of daily life, offering tailored solutions that cater to individual needs and preferences. Users can receive personalized advice by specifying the requirements and context, from organizing a day's activities to planning meals and choosing new books to explore. These examples showcase the versatility of ChatGPT in enhancing personal productivity and leisure, proving that with the right prompts, the boundaries of AI assistance expand continually.

Prompts for Learning and Development

The art of crafting prompts for educational purposes harnesses the expansive knowledge base and adaptability of ChatGPT, turning it into a personal tutor, guide, and source of inspiration. The prompts shown below are examples of how specific, well-thought-out prompts can significantly enhance the learning experience and offer personalized educational content, pathways to development of skills, and more.

Mastering a new language. "Can you provide a daily learning plan for a beginner to learn the Spanish language, focusing on vocabulary, grammar, and conversational phrases? Include interactive exercises and quizzes for self-evaluation."

Improving programming skills. "I'm familiar with the basics of Python. Could you suggest a project-based learning path that includes intermediate to advanced concepts, with examples and resources for hands-on practice?"

Exercising creative writing. "Offer a series of creative writing prompts with each exploring a genre, including mystery, science fiction, and autobiographical writing. Each prompt should aim to develop character building and plot structuring skills."

Analyzing historical events. "Create a list of pivotal historical events from the twentieth century, and provide a framework for analyzing their causes and consequences and the lessons learned from them. Include guiding questions for each event to encourage critical thinking."

Guiding art appreciation. "Develop a weekly art appreciation guide for six weeks consecutive weeks that covers various art movements, key figures, and their most iconic works. Incorporate interactive elements such as virtual museum tours and recommendations for artist documentaries to read or view."

By engaging with ChatGPT through tailored prompts such as these, an individual can embark on a process of self-improvement and knowledge acquisition that is both structured and flexible. Such prompts are designed to stimulate curiosity, encourage active participation, and facilitate deeper understanding, covering a broad spectrum of subjects from language learning and coding to creative expression and historical inquiry. Through this personalized approach to learning and development, ChatGPT can enrich the educational landscape, empowering users to pursue their interests and expand their horizons with unparalleled support.

Prompts for Entertainment and Leisure

ChatGPT, with its vast repository of knowledge and cultural insights, emerges as an ideal companion for venturing into uncharted territories of hobbies and interests. By crafting precise prompts, users can unlock personalized recommendations and ideas that resonate with their curiosity and preferences. The examples presented below unveil how ChatGPT can be a gateway to new adventures in entertainment and leisure, offering a pathway to hobbies and experiences that await discovery.

Discovering new hobbies. "I want to look into new hobbies that combine outdoor activities with technology. Can you suggest some unique hobbies that fit this description, including the equipment I will need and how to get started?"

Recommending a book to fit the user's mood. "I'm in the mood for an uplifting and inspiring book, possibly with a strong female lead. What are the top five books you recommend that fit these criteria, and why do you think they'll be a good match for me?"

Exploring culture through cinema. "Provide me with a list of five movies, each set in a different country and each with deep cultural insights, making sure each film comes from a distinct part of the world. Include a brief description of the cultural elements each movie explores."

Discovering relaxing music. "I'm searching for calming music that helps with relaxation. Can you recommend playlists or albums across genres known for their soothing qualities, and explain what makes each selection relaxing?"

Crafting and DIY projects. "I'm interested in starting a DIY project focused on sustainability and upcycling. Can you suggest a project that beginners can handle, detailing the materials needed and the steps involved?"

Through prompts such as these, ChatGPT can act as a pathway to a world brimming with possibilities, guiding users toward finding joy in new hobbies, books, films, music, and crafting projects. Each suggestion ignites interest, catering to users' diverse tastes and inclinations. ChatGPT is ready to enhance your leisure and entertainment experience with personalized guidance and inspiration, from embracing the great outdoors with a tech twist, delving into uplifting literature, experiencing the richness of global cultures through cinema, finding solace in music, to looking into creative expression with DIY projects.

Prompts for Personal Well-Being

ChatGPT can become a companion on the path to personal well-being, offering customizable support tailored to individual needs and lifestyles. The example prompts shown below for mental health exercises, meditation, physical activity, nutrition, or sleep hygiene, are designed to inspire and facilitate positive changes.

Checking mental health. "Can you guide me through a weekly mental health check-in? Include questions that help me reflect on my emotional state, stress levels, and happiness, and offer tips for how to improve my mental well-being."

Customizing meditation. "Create a 10-minute meditation routine tailored for beginners. Please provide step-by-step instructions that focus on mindfulness and stress reduction, suitable for starting my day."

Designing an exercise routine to fit a busy schedule. "Design a twenty-minute exercise routine that can be done at home with no equipment. It should target all major muscle groups and suit someone with a busy schedule who wants to stay active."

Creating a healthy eating plan. "Create a seven-day healthy eating plan that balances nutrients and flavors. Include meal and snack ideas that are simple to prepare, focusing on whole foods and incorporating plenty of fruits and vegetables."

Improving sleep quality and promoting unwinding. "Offer advice on improving sleep quality for someone struggling to unwind at night. Suggest a bedtime routine that promotes relaxation, and provide tips for creating an ideal sleep environment."

By engaging with ChatGPT in this manner, users can harness the power of AI to achieve and maintain optimal health and well-being, while emphasizing the profound impact of personalized guidance on the quest for a balanced and healthy life.

Prompts for Small Businesses

In the bustling world of small businesses, exceptional customer support stands as a pillar of success. It's not just about answering questions; it's about building relationships, trust, and a lasting reputation. ChatGPT, with its conversational prowess, offers small business owners a powerful tool to revolutionize their customer support systems. By crafting precise prompts, businesses can generate comprehensive FAQ responses, create engaging customer service scripts, and more, ensuring every customer interaction is meaningful and effective.

Responding to FAQs. "Generate a detailed FAQ response for 'What is your return policy?' including steps for return, time frame, and condition of products accepted."

Creating customer service scripts for product inquiries. "Create a customer service script for handling inquiries about product specifications, incorporating polite greetings, questions to gain understanding of customer needs, and closing statements that encourage purchase."

Handling negative feedback. "Draft a response script for addressing customer complaints about delayed shipments, focusing on empathy, explanation of the delay, and the actions taken to resolve the issue."

Producing live chat greeting messages. "Produce a set of welcoming messages for live chat support that convey warmth and readiness to assist, tailored for morning, afternoon, and evening interactions."

Formulating guidelines for escalating customer issues. "Formulate a step-by-step guide for customer service representatives on escalating unresolved customer issues, including criteria for escalation, internal communication, and follow-up procedures."

These prompts, created with clarity and specificity, enable small businesses to leverage ChatGPT to create a customer support framework that is efficient and deeply attuned to the needs and concerns of their clientele. Through the strategic use of ChatGPT, businesses can ensure that every customer interaction is handled with care, precision, and a personal touch, reinforcing the values that define the heart and soul of small enterprises. This approach streamlines customer support operations and fosters an environment where customer satisfaction is paramount, driving loyalty and business growth.

Prompts for Content Creation

In the bustling digital marketplace, content is the currency that connects businesses with their audiences, weaving stories that engage, inform, and inspire. As small businesses strive to carve out their niches, creating compelling content becomes paramount. ChatGPT emerges as an invaluable chatbot in this creative endeavor, offering a wellspring of ideas and narratives tailored to a brand's voice and vision. By employing precise and thoughtfully crafted prompts, small businesses can harness ChatGPT's capabilities to generate blog posts, social media content, and marketing materials that resonate with their target audience.

Generating ideas for blog posts. "Generate five innovative blog post ideas for a sustainable living blog, focusing on zero-waste practices. Include suggested titles, a brief outline for each post, and key messages to convey."

Creating social media content for a product launch. "Create a series of five engaging social media posts to promote the launch of an eco-friendly kitchen product. Each post should highlight a different feature of the product and include a call to action encouraging followers to learn more."

Developing an email marketing campaign for a seasonal sale. "Draft an email marketing campaign for a seasonal sale in a boutique clothing store. The campaign should include three emails: a teaser for the upcoming sale, an official announcement with sale details, and a last-chance reminder. Focus on creating a compelling narrative that emphasizes the uniqueness and quality of the collection."

Incorporating a customer testimonial feature into a website. "Outline a format for featuring customer testimonials on a service-based business website. Include prompts for collecting testimonials that capture the customer's experience and the impact of the service provided."

Generating infographic content for health and wellness tips. "Propose content for an infographic offering health and wellness tips for remote workers. Highlight five key tips that promote physical health, mental well-being, and productivity. Include a catchy headline and a brief explanation for each tip."

Through these prompts, ChatGPT becomes a creative partner, enabling small businesses to craft content that captivates while adding value to their audience's lives. Whether it's through insightful blog posts, vibrant social media campaigns, personalized email marketing, authentic customer stories, or informative infographics, the content created with ChatGPT's assistance stands out in a crowded digital landscape. This approach to content creation fosters deeper connections with existing customers and attracts new ones, driving growth and building a loyal community around the brand. By leveraging the power of AI in their content strategy, small businesses can navigate the complexities of the digital world with confidence, creativity, and a clear voice that speaks directly to the hearts and minds of their audience.

Prompts for Improving Operational Efficiency

In the dynamic environment of small businesses, operational efficiency isn't just an objective; it's the backbone that supports growth, sustainability, and success. The integration of artificial intelligence, particularly ChatGPT, into business operations offers unparalleled opportunities to streamline operations, from project management to inventory tracking. By formulating targeted prompts, businesses can unlock actionable insights and solutions, propelling them toward optimal operational performance. This exploration into the realm of operational efficiency through ChatGPT demonstrates the transformative potential of AI in the operational aspects of small businesses.

Optimizing project management. "Can you create a comprehensive project management plan for a small team working on a digital marketing campaign? Include milestones, task assignments, and deadlines, ensuring a balance in workload distribution."

Tracking inventory. "Develop a straightforward inventory tracking system for a boutique clothing store that categorizes items by type, size, and color. Include prompts for updating stock levels and flagging items for restocking."

Strategizing customer relationship management. "Outline a strategy for managing customer relationships in a small service-based business, incorporating methods for tracking client interactions, feedback, and follow-up activities."

Designing efficient workflow design for remote teams. "Suggest an efficient workflow design for a remote team, focusing on communication, task allocation, and progress tracking. Highlight tools and practices that enhance collaboration and minimize delays."

Cost reduction analysis. "Generate a prompt for conducting a cost reduction analysis in a small manufacturing business. Include steps for identifying areas of high expenditure, evaluating alternative suppliers, and optimizing production processes for cost savings."

Through these prompts, ChatGPT becomes an essential tool in the quest for operational excellence, offering innovative and practical solutions. Small businesses can leverage these AI-generated strategies to improve project management, refine inventory systems, cultivate customer relationships, streamline workflows, and analyze costs effectively. In doing so, they boost their operational efficiency and set the stage for sustained growth and competitiveness in their respective markets. Operational optimization, guided by ChatGPT, exemplifies the synergy between human ingenuity and artificial intelligence, heralding a new era of efficiency and effectiveness in the small business sector.

Prompts for Market Analysis and Strategy

In the competitive arena of small business, understanding the market landscape and carving out a strategic position is not just beneficial—it's imperative for survival and growth. The advent of AI technologies like ChatGPT provides an edge in these endeavors, offering small businesses insights and strategies that were once the domain of market research firms. By engaging ChatGPT with targeted prompts, small businesses can conduct comprehensive competitive analysis, delve into market research, and craft strategies that propel them ahead of the curve. The following examples show how ChatGPT can be pivotal in deciphering market dynamics and informing strategic decisions.

Analyzing competition via deep dives. "Generate a detailed competitive analysis for a boutique coffee shop in a metropolitan area. Focus on direct competitors' product offerings, pricing strategies, customer service approaches, and online presence."

Forecasting market trends. "Identify and describe the top five emerging trends in the organic skincare industry for the next year. Include potential impacts on consumer preferences and how small businesses can adapt to these trends."

Segmenting customers for targeted marketing. "Outline a customer segmentation strategy for an online educational platform. Categorize potential customers based on demographics, interests, and learning goals to tailor marketing messages and course offerings."

Conducting a SWOT analysis for strategic planning. "Conduct a SWOT analysis (an analysis of strengths, weaknesses, opportunities, and threats) for a small tech startup, focusing on renewable energy solutions. Highlight key areas for growth and potential challenges in the current market environment."

Creating a product positioning strategy. "Create a product positioning strategy for a new vegan snack line. Consider unique selling propositions, target customer demographics, and messaging that differentiates the product from existing options in the market."

Through the use of prompts similar to those set forth in this chapter, small businesses can rely on ChatGPT as an invaluable tool in navigating the complex world of market analysis and strategic planning. Small businesses can leverage this AI-powered assistance to understand their competitive landscapes, anticipate market shifts, tailor their offerings to meet customers needs, and position themselves strategically within their industries. This proactive approach to market analysis and strategy formulation underscores the transformative potential of AI in empowering small businesses to make informed decisions, adapt to changing market conditions, and carve out a path to success.

Effective prompt crafting is akin to effectively steering a ship: the more precise the directions, the smoother the voyage to the destination. Crafting useful prompts requires having an understanding of the AI's capabilities and limitations, a creative mind to navigate various formulations, and the patience to refine and iterate. This process is not about commanding a digital assistant but engaging in a dynamic dialogue wherein each prompt is a question, a request, or a challenge that invites ChatGPT to explore into its depths and bring forth informative, insightful, innovative responses.

The variety of prompts presented in this chapter is a testament to the versatility of ChatGPT. From organizing daily tasks and fostering personal well-being to crafting marketing strategies and analyzing competitive landscapes, the potential applications are as vast as the user's imagination. However, the true magic comes from customizing these prompts further to meet specific needs and contexts. Each individual and business has unique challenges and goals. By tailoring prompts to these unique scenarios, ChatGPT can provide solutions that are not only effective but also highly personalized.

Try your own experiments with ChatGPT. Don't shy away from going into detail with your prompts. View each interaction as an opportunity to learn and refine your approach. The process is iterative and exploratory, with each attempt providing insights into how best to communicate with the AI to achieve desired outcomes. Simplifying a complex problem? Seeking creative inspiration? Looking for data-driven insights? How questions are framed can significantly influence the effectiveness of the responses received.

This experimentation highlights the importance of a collaborative approach to AI interactions. ChatGPT, with its evolving capabilities, is a tool that grows and learns from each exchange. Users are both beneficiaries of this technology and active participants in its development, contributing to the collective understanding of how best to leverage AI in our daily lives and work.

The art of prompt crafting is an essential skill for the modern age, a key that unlocks the full potential of ChatGPT. By understanding the principles of effective prompt design, individuals and businesses can harness the power of AI to access new horizons, solve complex challenges, and create value in innovative and efficient ways. The invitation stands for all to experiment, adapt, and innovate with prompts, shaping the future of AI interaction in ways that enrich both personal and professional realms. The technology within ChatGPT is just beginning, and the possibilities are limitless.

Final Words

Throughout this book, we've explored the vast capabilities of ChatGPT, a groundbreaking AI tool designed to streamline and revolutionize how we approach personal tasks and business operations.

The core insights of this exploration revolve around the practical applications of ChatGPT in streamlining workflow processes, automating repetitive tasks, and providing innovative solutions to complex problems. We have delved into the art of crafting effective prompts, a critical skill for harnessing the full potential of ChatGPT, ensuring that users can communicate their needs precisely to receive the most relevant and helpful responses.

One of the pivotal strategies we've highlighted is the customization of ChatGPT to fit individual or business-specific needs ranging from content creation and customer service to project management and data analysis, showcasing its flexibility across various industries. This adaptability underscores ChatGPT's role as a versatile resource in navigating the challenges of the digital age.

We have also emphasized the importance of ethical considerations and responsible use of AI technologies. By fostering an understanding of ChatGPT's capabilities and limitations, we have given you the knowledge to use this technology wisely to enhance your productivity while adhering to ethical standards.

Before reading this book, you may have perceived ChatGPT as merely a novel technology, perhaps intriguing, yet distant from your daily realities. However, by engaging with practical exercises, real-world examples, and the step-by-step instructions within this book, we hope the formerly abstract concept of AI has become tangible, its applications clear, and its benefits undeniable.

As we close the pages of *ChatGPT Essentials for Beginners,* we encourage you not to let your investigation into AI end here. This book has armed you with the knowledge and tools to revolutionize your everyday life and small business operations through ChatGPT. Now, it's time to get started! The true potential of what you've learned can be realized only through application and experimentation. Start with small projects or tasks you wish to optimize or automate.

Embrace the mindset of continuous learning and experimentation. The field of AI and technologies like ChatGPT are evolving rapidly, offering new possibilities and opportunities. Stay curious, stay informed, and don't hesitate to experiment with new prompts and applications as you grow more comfortable and proficient with ChatGPT.

Remember, every significant change begins with a single step. Let the insights from this book be the catalyst for your transformation. Apply the strategies, explore your potential with AI, and witness the profound impact ChatGPT can have on your life and work. The future is in your hands, and with ChatGPT, you're equipped to shape it. So, take the leap, start experimenting, and transform your world, one prompt at a time.

To navigate this promising yet uncertain future, it's crucial to be informed and adaptable. Engage with the AI community, follow the latest research and developments, and remain open to exploring new tools and technologies as they emerge. By doing so, you will be well-positioned to leverage the opportunities of this dynamic landscape, ensuring a future where AI, with ChatGPT at the forefront, is a powerful ally in realizing your fullest potential.

In the words of accomplished American computer scientist Alan Kay, "The best way to predict the future is to invent it." This book is an invitation to you—not just to anticipate the future of AI and technology but to actively shape it through your actions and innovations. Let ChatGPT be your companion in this endeavor, a tool that empowers you to redefine the boundaries of what is possible.

So, as you move forward, carry with you the insights, strategies, and inspiration gleaned from these pages. Experiment boldly, learn continuously, and let your knowledge of ChatGPT be a testament to the remarkable capabilities that emerge when human creativity meets the power of AI.

About the author

James Gilbert, 27, navigates life with the spirit of an adventurer. Born to a Spanish mother and English father, he grew up in South America and attended a British international school in Peru. As a digital nomad, he pursues his passions for skydiving and game fishing in his free time. Fluent in Spanish, English, and Aymaran, James bridges cultures and experiences seamlessly into his writing. A master of generative AI, web design, and marketing, he aims to inspire readers to harness the power of technology and embark on their own adventures. James's unique background and dynamic lifestyle infuse his work with a distinctive perspective, making complex concepts accessible and engaging.

Made in the USA
Monee, IL
04 November 2026

67379937R00059